His Rest

Is Glorious

Reaching The Anointing
That Arrests All Fear

His Rest

Is Glorious

All Scriptures taken from the King James Bible

Blessings to all who supported the completion of this assignment
Estelle Taylor and W.C.T.T.P., Joyce Taylor, Joyce Shipley, Bob and
Ann McMahon, Barney L. Christie, Anthony Christie, Margaret Brown
and the Prayer Clinic Team

And in that day there shall be a root of Jesse, which shall stand for an ensign **[A SIGN, A STANDARD]** of the people; to it **[HIM/JESUS]** shall the Gentiles seek:

<u>and his rest shall be glorious.</u>

Isaiah 11:10

Table of Contents

Foreword	5
Preface	6
Introduction	8
Meditation	10
Knowledge Invasion	11
Order and Rest	15
So You've been in a War	19
Thy Kingdom Come	21
Fear is Unconstitutional (Order in the Court!)	23
Take My Yoke	25
Meditation	26
Rest: The Root Solution	27
His Rest is Glorious	33
Anxiety (The Current of Unrest)	38
Rest and The Sabbath Day	41
Meditation	44
Prophetic Dependence	45
Prophetic Assignments (Elijah)	47
Prophetic Confrontation	49
Prophetic Declaration	51
Prophetic Demonstration	53
Weakness and Rest	55
God of Elijah, Elijah of God	58
Meditation	62
REST: The weapon of divine positioning over Death	63
Breaking Fears Dominion	66
2 More Dimensions of Protection	68
What is a Knowledge Trap?	72
16 Ways to Defeat a Knowledge Trap	92
Meditation	107
R.E.A.C.H.	108
Conclusions in Rest	112
Author's addt'l notes	115
Under The Shadow	118

FOREWORD

Though it is not common for an author to write his or her own Forward, due to the nature of this book's content, and the basis for this volume, I was compelled to write my own. His Rest Is Glorious is as much the testimony of my encounter with Him, and His Rest, as it is a description of the Glorious Anointing and Dominion of The Lord Jesus Christ in Isaiah 11:10. My encounter with His Rest revolutionized my life, and forever broke my captivity to Fear. Now I know and am certain that there is a living and glorious substance readily available and accessible to all mankind, everywhere, if they will come to Jesus for Rest. This substance apprehends FEAR and neutralizes it immediately! This substance is a Kingdom Dominion, and an all powerful anointing that flows from The Anointed One, Christ himself. He is as accessible today, as he was when he was here in the earth. As you read this volume, Rest will begin to manifest, but this is just a roadmap...Reach for the Anointed One yourself, he is releasing His Rest to those who will come, and destroying all of their fears. This Rest is not a natural practice, or a spiritual concept, nor is it a teaching platform (though we will teach on the subject of Rest and Fear), no, this Rest is as real as the air we breathe, or the blood that courses through our veins, or water that streams from a shower head... It must indeed be that real, that tangible, in order to arrest the criminal FEAR.

PREFACE

Have you ever suffered a Life Invasion? The place of your greatest rest and security trespassed and breached by brutal, lawless criminals. Your conscience bruised, and your soul battered...

Since the fall of man, the criminal FEAR has trespassed the human spirit, and invaded the human soul. Such success throughout the ages has made fear arrogant and brash, heartless and invasive. It relies primarily on impact, seizing any available opportunity to present or represent itself, and if at all possible, to enter into the human heart and torment...I recently visited a cancer center with a member of our assembly who was undergoing some blood tests. Thanks be to God, they were all negative! It was then that I ran into a cancer patient in the hallway, a young woman of about 40 years of age. As our eyes met, I asked her how she was doing, and cautiously she replied that she was learning to cope with her disease. What she said next, moved me to release this book ahead of my next book, and I quote "it's not the cancer that's killing me, it's the FEAR". After hearing this, I immediately began to both break the power of fear by the Rest and Authority of Jesus Christ, and to administer his healing virtue.

One of the greatest tools that fear uses is *Knowledge*. It needs a point of reference from which to torment, magnify and manipulate our mental, physical and emotional beings. Much like the first Knowledge Trap, Adam wasn't afraid of nakedness, until he was "told" that he was naked. We will look into Knowledge Traps, and how they work in the coming chapters.

I can hear the Holy Spirit speaking within me now, saying "Who told you that it's incurable, impossible or irreversible"... "Have you eaten from the Tree of the Knowledge of Good and Evil"?

In order to break through the threshold of the impossible, one will almost always have to walk down the hallway of fear. In the coming chapters we are going to teach you how to enter the Dominion of Rest, defeat a Knowledge Trap, and remain protected from Fear. If the truth be told, the brokers of fear (demons and the long list of propagators of knowledge based fear) are trembling now as His Rest goes forth to defeat and neutralize Fear.

...and his rest shall be glorious. **Isaiah 11:10**

INTRODUCTION

When Adam was formed, God's creation was at Rest, man's existence was without chaos..., his life was without Fear. In Genesis Chapter 2 we see God breathing and releasing into man His very Spirit and Breath. Adam walked and lived in this place of rest, under this anointing of rest, for an undisclosed period of time, and never knew unrest until the day that he chose Knowledge over Life. *"The day that thou eatest thereof (knowledge) you shall surely die"* (Genesis 2:17) The first recorded instance of fear, followed the first recorded instance of sin and death (separation from God). It paralyzed and flustered Adam, so much so, that he fled from the presence of his very best friend, his Designer, Architect, and Creator. The fear of nakedness, the fear of death. the fear of rejection, even the fear of God's presence, all entered in at that very moment.

What was it that interrupted the sweet and intimate fellowship that Adam had with the Lord? What was it that caused Adam to experience such a gut wrenching sense of emptiness and nakedness, which for Adam, produced great fear? We know that fear came in as a result of sin and separation, but what gave it such an immediate and unprecedented snare within the heart and mind of Adam, who had for his entire life known nothing but peace and security? As we endeavor to answer this question, we will most assuredly gain invaluable insight into how fear works.

The Devil is not the author of fear, the power behind fear, nor is he the one who told Adam that he was naked.

And when the woman saw that the tree was good for food, and that it was pleasant to the eyes, and a tree to be desired to make one wise, she took of the fruit thereof, and did eat, and gave also unto her husband with her; and he did eat. ***And the eyes of them both were opened, and they knew that they were naked;***

So who was the culprit..., who told Adam that he was naked?

And they heard the voice of the LORD God walking in the garden in the cool of the day: and Adam and his wife hid themselves from the presence of the LORD God amongst the trees of the garden. And the LORD God called unto Adam, and said unto him, ***Where art thou****? And he (Adam) said, I heard thy voice in the garden, and I was afraid, because I was naked; and I hid myself.*

Genesis 3:6-10

The eyes of mankind were forever opened, unseated from the position of rest, removed from his habitation, invaded by fear, and separated from ingenerate life.

Though Adam tried to hide, he wasn't ever really hidden from God, his condition was far more critical than that; he had been separated from God. As God momentarily turned His attention away from Adam, He did not immediately implicate the Serpent in this assault on mankind, but pointed to unfiltered knowledge as the source of Adam's unrest!

MEDITATION

The next few chapters are intended to lay the foundation

- That mankind was created in and for Rest

- That this Rest is directly connected to Order, Power and Authority in the Kingdom of God, Resulting in Soundness in the human experience

- That Unfiltered Knowledge can wreak havoc on the soul

- That Fear has no Dominion in the Kingdom of God, and thus, should have no Dominion within the lives of believers today

- That Unbridled Fear has just hit a brick wall, and can go no further...This brick wall is the Rest of God

THE KNOWLEDGE INVASION

Having dealt with fear for much of my life, I have become very familiar with its methods. Fear is uncreative, yet very resilient; it does not reinvent itself and has only one objective, to move us out of the Kingdom of God, and out of the order of that Kingdom! Fear is not a being; it is a realm of knowledge that is utilized by demonic beings. When we refer to a "spirit of fear" we are really referring to a spirit (whether demon or principality) that utilizes Fear as a weapon, and/or the human spirit/soul that has been affected by the presence of such an assignment against the heart and mind. Some people are known for walking in, carrying, or being sensitive to the "spirit of fear". In Genesis 2:17 God warns Adam and Eve not to eat from the "tree of the knowledge of good and evil", because the result would be death or separation from Himself, and ultimately separation from Rest. After the events of Genesis 3:6-7, mankind would never again take for granted the Dominion of Rest.

And when the woman saw that the tree was good for food, and that it was pleasant to the eyes, and a tree to be desired to make one wise, she took of the fruit thereof, and did eat, and gave also unto her husband with her; and he did eat. And the eyes of them both were opened, and they knew that they were naked; and they sewed fig leaves together, and made themselves aprons. And they heard the voice of the LORD God walking in the garden in the cool of the day: and Adam and his wife hid themselves from the presence of the LORD God amongst the trees of the garden.

Genesis 3:6-8

All of a sudden, the Rest was gone, and Fear had rushed in and taken immediate dominion within the realm of man's soul. The serpent gained his initial understanding of man's vulnerability to fear by observation. He was there in the garden. He had seduced them into eating from the wrong tree. He saw the way Adam responded to knowledge, and how he greatly feared it. He was an eyewitness to man's first area of fallen weakness, fear capitalizing on knowledge.

"I was afraid, <u>because I was naked</u>" **Genesis 3:10**

Or we could say it this way, *"I was afraid, because I discovered that I was naked".* Adam had always been naked, *but* nakedness was new to Adam, and he didn't need to know it. Man's initial experience with fear came as result of the enemy baiting him into a relationship with knowledge. Every good hunter knows how to lay the bait for his prey. In Adam's case, he walked right into a Knowledge Trap. In order to understand the power of knowledge, we must understand how the soul of man works.

Our Souls are comprised of (4) compartments, the mind, the intellect, the will and the emotions. I believe that Adam was being trained by the Lord to live after his spirit, and not after his soul. Had he waited on God's timing until he was spiritually trained to filter all knowledge (discerning by the spirit), and remained free from sins dominion, he may have eventually been able to eat from the Tree of Knowledge without harm. I have recently learned to apply filters within my soul, when ingesting new forms of knowledge. Such filters as faith, love and wisdom (God's Word) have allowed me to remain in the Rest of God, steer clear of knowledge traps, and stay out of the snare of fear.

The (natural) mind (which is in the soul) is like the hard drive in a computer that collects information and stores it away as thoughts, both conscious and subconscious. The (carnal) intellect (which is in the soul) is more like the CPU, it processes the thoughts collected, and can come to conclusions by reasoning and sometimes by logic (calculating learned facts and information). God Himself taught Adam all that he needed, and only what he was ready to know; filtering, straining, pureeing and purifying every once of Truth with Love.

Without such filtering, even a seemingly simple concept like nakedness brought immense fear and trepidation to Adam. This knowledge wasn't measured in Grace, spoken in Love, or delivered in Wisdom. God's Word, being the highest form of Wisdom, always trumps the wisdom of men and trees! Oh that we would carefully consider the potential of unfiltered knowledge to rattle our souls…; and filter all knowledge with the Word of God!

Whenever we receive new information, it is often the intellect (which is in the soul) that processes it. In some cases, the spiritual man or woman is better off knowing as little as possible about a challenging situation they may have to face, until they have taken in the LIFE of God's Spirit and Word, so that they might filter all incoming knowledge with God's Promises (birthed by LOVE). Our wills (within our souls) choose to receive or to reject incoming forms of knowledge, and while the human will is a very powerful force, in many cases, it is the influence of the emotions that fight to rule within the soul, especially when a person is confronted with fear. One great example of living out of the spirit, and filtering incoming knowledge, was in the case of Daniel, in the Lions' Den. Daniel, who knew to fear Lions, filtered that knowledge with faith in his God, and obtained a testimony over death!

My God hath sent his angel, and hath shut the lions' mouths, that they have not hurt me: **Daniel 6:22**

And he (God) said, ***"Who told thee that thou wast naked?*** *Hast thou eaten of the tree, whereof I commanded thee that thou shouldest not eat?"* **Genesis 3:11**

Yes, knowledge is everywhere, and comes in many forms. The Tree of Knowledge began mankind's affair with the realm of limitations, and knowledge based fears. Absolute Truth, on the other hand, can only be found in one place...Jesus Christ...The Word of God. As you continue to read, you will be reconciled to the One who gives us Rest and Order, repositions us emotionally, mentally and spiritually. This Jesus Christ, The Word of God, is the Last Adam..., he has come to restore what the first Adam lost!

ORDER AND REST

Rest is essential to man's composition

In Genesis Chapter 1, we have the account of Creation.

In the beginning God <u>created</u> the heaven and the earth. And the earth was <u>without form</u>, and void; and darkness was upon the face of the deep. And the Spirit of God moved upon the face of the waters.   **Genesis   1:1**

Here we see that God created the earth, but had not yet formed it. It, the earth, was created, and yet for a short period it remained void and without form. With God, creation happens, with or without formation. When He speaks by the creative power of His Word, something is always happening in the unseen realm. In the next few verses we begin to see the earth taking form.

And God said, Let the waters under the heaven be gathered together unto one place, and let the dry land appear: and it was so. And God called the dry land Earth; and the gathering together of the waters called he Seas: and God saw that it was good. And God said, Let the earth bring forth grass, the herb yielding seed...

Genesis 1:9-11

After creating the earth, God did not leave the earth in a

void state, but formed it according to his own pleasure. We see this very same pattern with mankind.

...I will give thanks to You, for I am fearfully and wonderfully made; Wonderful are Your works, And my soul knows it very well. My frame was not hidden from You, When I was made in secret, ... Your eyes have seen my unformed substance;

Psalms 139:14-16

The truth that before we were formed in our mother's womb, God framed us and knew us, is a common truth in scripture. Here, the psalmist rests in the truth that he was known, before he was formed, and that God's eyes had seen his unformed substance. He was not the product of chance, evolution or random spontaneity, and this truth brought the psalmist great rest. In like manner, when Adam was created, God knew his frame, and the potential frailty of his soul, he was gloriously designed, fearfully and wonderfully made. When God breathed into Adam of His very Life and Spirit, there was not one iota of fear imparted, because God is love, perfect Love, unparalleled Love, unbridled Love. He, who is Love, knows no Fear. Adam was created to have a fearless existence just like God, living before God, and abiding in God's Rest... Let's take a closer look at the Rest of God.

It is my belief that we have overlooked this amazing phenomenon called the REST OF GOD. It is curious at best that God rested at all (**Genesis 2:1-3**). Why would the Almighty God need to rest? I am assured in my heart that it is not because He was exhausted from His labors. Perhaps it was because He wanted to contemplate the good which He had created, or to give man a pattern of rest to follow. These all ring true, and yet I believe that a great mystery is staring us right in the face.   I believe that REST is the Order of the Kingdom of God, The Divine Position, The Place of Absolute Authority, Power and Rule. When God sits upon the Throne of His Glory, He orders all things from a position of REST! Within God's Kingdom there is no unrest, and all things are subject to Him. All things subdued by the Right Hand of His power, neutralized by the Dominion of Rest! When God resorted to Rest in Genesis Chapter 2, He resorted to the Divine Position...Seated at His Throne. I believe that this REST (the position and presence) was being established in the earth for Adam, just as it was in Heaven.

For an undetermined amount of time, all Adam knew was God's Love, Glory and Rest. Living was easy, his life was in order, divinely positioned, and completely surrounded by Glory. Adam had a fearless existence before God!

*And the LORD God said, It is not good that the man should be alone; I will make him an help meet for him. And the LORD God caused a **deep sleep to fall upon Adam**, and he slept: and he took one of his ribs, and closed up the flesh instead thereof; And the rib, which the LORD God had taken from man, made he a woman, and brought her unto the man. And Adam said, This is now bone of my bones, and flesh of my flesh: she* *shall be called Woman, because she was taken out of Man. There-fore shall a man leave his father and his mother, and shall cleave unto his wife: and they shall be one flesh. And they were both na-ked, the man and his wife, and were not ashamed.*

Genesis 2:18-25

Even the formation of Eve seemed to involve God's Rest, as a deep sleep came upon Adam. A rib being taken from the rest-ing Adam to *form* her in REST, and bring her back to her husband equally yoked in the Rest of God. *Bone of his bone and flesh of his flesh.*

The Rest and Breath of God was mankind's first inheri-tance, and was to be a part of his very substance. This Rest was in full dominion over Adam's spirit, soul and body. Even their living quarters, Eden, *meaning* paradise or bliss, was a type of Heaven, the Throne of God, a Resting place.

*Thus said the LORD, The heaven is my throne, and the earth is my footstool: where is the house that you build to me? and **where is the place of my rest?*** **Isaiah 66:1**

The Lord here suggests that he already has a recliner in Heaven, and a footstool in Earth that no man can improve upon. Nevertheless, He is calling a people in this day, who will come to Jesus Christ and become the very sanctuary of His Rest.

Come unto me, all ye that labour and are heavy laden, and I will give you rest **Matthew 11:28**

SO YOU'VE BEEN IN A WAR

Rest is the Game Changer

For every battle of the warrior is with confused noise, and garments rolled in blood; but this shall be with burning and fuel of fire.   **Isaiah 9:5**

This is a powerful and accurate description of the actualities of natural and spiritual war, and while it is an absolute truth that we (The Body of Christ) are on the winning side, and that the outcome is fixed, the battle still rages on! The inference in the above scripture is that of a WAR that escalates and increases in intensity *"with burning and fuel of fire"*... This is the WAR SCENARIO for the End-Times, *there shall be "wars and rumors of wars" Matthew 24:6* thus, the Father is providing High-Level Training and Equipping for His Saints in these evil days.

While our Father's Love remains a Strong Tower for us, and His Kingdom, Power and Glory are unparalleled, He is quite deliberately preparing a people to stand, and strengthening a people to overcome in these last days! Uncommon, are the weapons of our WARFARE; OTHER-WORLDLY are the methods of our God! In the natural realm, these weapons can only be compared to a Nuclear Arsenal. They are unparalleled in power, game-changers, catastrophic to alien armies, preserving and establishing the Domicile of the Kingdom of God and its people, wherever and whenever they are used. These weapons are being distributed to end-time soldiers, sons and daughters, intent upon standing in the Evil Day! The Lord is equipping his people to be able to STAND! One of the major battle stands in the end-times will be against a Principality called FEAR!

For we wrestle not against flesh and blood but against principalities... **Ephesians 6:12**

(A principality is a ruler in the realms of darkness, usually over a region, but occasionally, one may be assigned to an individual.)

PRAYER: I take dominion and authority over every assignment of fear against your life. I break fears power over your spirit and soul by the authority of the Lord Jesus Christ, and release to you the dominion of Rest (which is in Jesus Christ). **Declare this with me:** I receive the Rest of the Lord Jesus Christ. I receive the Rest of the Lord Jesus Christ.

REACH for the Rest of the Lord Jesus Christ. I declare the Dominion of Rest over you in the name of the Lord Jesus Christ! I inject you with the substance of Rest in the name of the Lord Jesus Christ; breaking and neutralizing fear and anxiety by Rest and by Peace...These are two of the most powerful Kingdom Dominions! These are realms of absolute authority that God establishes in the lives of believers, in regions, and in environments. Be established in Rest...and Reach for Jesus NOW!

THY KINGDOM COME

Jesus is the Warrior–King of Glory, The Captain of the Hosts, and the God of the Angel-Armies. His WAR-ROBE is a Garment dipped in Blood, his name is the Word of God, and upon his back is a name written, King of Kings and Lord of Lords!!! **Rev 19:13-16** (*see Gall: Overcoming the Power of Dominating Emotions "A Vesture Dipped in Blood"*)

The Blood, here, is more than a symbol, it is an Agent of Righteousness [A KINGDOM DOMINION]. This Kingdom Dominion called Righteousness is a Force to be reckoned with. It is a Pillar in the Kingdom of God, a place of Rule and Absolute Authority. It Represents Christ's character and actions, his judgments and motivations for WAR! He is the Righteous One!

And I saw heaven opened, and behold a white horse; and he that sat upon him was called Faithful and True, **and in righteousness he doth judge and make war.**

Revelation 19:11

If you are a believer in Jesus Christ begin now to declare his Righteousness over your life and know that Jesus is warring for you in prayer and intercession against the rule of fear in your life! **Declare this with me: Thy Kingdom Come in my life Heavenly Father, In Jesus name!**

The Kingdom Dominion of PEACE

For unto us a child is born, unto us a son is given: and the government shall be upon his shoulder: and his name shall be called Wonderful, Counsellor, The mighty God, The everlasting Father, The Prince of Peace.   **Isaiah 9:6**

This JESUS, the Prince of Peace, is not a peace-keeper, he is a PEACE MAKER, creating atmospheres and establishing Dominions by neutralizing everything that opposes Peace. This Peace is so powerful, that it has become synonymous with his Kingdom, and like His Kingdom, it is ever-increasing and eternal! Family of God, let it be known that this is no ordinary peace, this is no earthly substance, this is no realm of emotion, this is **a KINGDOM DO-MINION!**

*Of the increase of his government and peace there shall be no end, upon the throne of David, and upon his kingdom, to **order it**, and to **establish it** with judgment and with justice from henceforth even for ever. The zeal of the LORD of hosts will perform this.*   **Isaiah 9:6,7**

There are two main things that Christ's Government and Peace do wherever they are found: They Bring Order & They Establish Justice and Judgment. **Declare this with me: Lord Jesus, you are bringing Order (Rest) into, and establishing Justice within my life. Therefore, I declare boldly, as a citizen of your Kingdom of Peace, that Fear has no dominion over me!**

ORDER IN THE COURT
FEAR IS UNCONSTITUTIONAL

The only fear resident within the Kingdom of Heaven is the reverential fear of God! Fear (as a terror) is alien to the Kingdom of God, it is against the Constitution of the Kingdom of Christ, and it is a product of the Tree of the Knowledge of Good and Evil. Ever since the fall of mankind, fear has been given unbridled dominion in the earth, and in the hearts of men. The enemy of our souls has used this to his own advantage, and has thereby wounded and tormented many precious saints of God.

Forasmuch then as the children are partakers of flesh and blood, he also himself likewise took part of the same; that through death he might destroy him that had the power of death, that is, the devil; And deliver them who through fear of death were all their lifetime subject to bondage... **Hebrews 2:14-15**

Jesus Christ suffered death that he might destroy him that had the power of Death, that is, the devil! That is awesome news!

1.) A judgment has been ruled against the devil

2.) The devil has been stripped of the power of death

3.) The law of sin and death has been destroyed for believers

4.) The gates of Hell shall not prevail against the believing ones

So why has the devil been able to keep so many in Bondage to the fear of death? Where is the deliverance that Jesus has provided for us? I've got news for you, it's been hidden in plain sight. Deliverance from all fear is available to every believer. Where is it you might ask? It's in Jesus Christ! Well before you complain about the answer: Remember the scripture:

And deliver them who through fear of death were all their lifetime subject to bondage.   **Hebrews 2:14-15**

The Lord Jesus Christ has destroyed him that had the power of death AND come to deliver all who suffer from the fear of Death. The Word Christ means the "Anointed One". This Jesus, the Son of God, The Prince of Peace, The Last Adam, has come to restore the Rest lost by the First Adam!

And so it is written, The first man Adam was made a living soul; the last Adam was made a quickening spirit.

1Corinthians 15:45

Even as God breathed His Spirit and Rest into Adam in the beginning of the creation/formation of man, Christ wants to breathe his Rest into us!

Come unto me, all ye that labour and are heavy laden, and I will give you rest. Take my yoke upon you, and learn of me; for I am meek and lowly in heart: and ye shall find rest unto your souls.   **Matthew 11:28-29**

TAKE MY YOKE

...Take my yoke upon you, and learn of me; for I am meek and lowly in heart: and ye shall find rest unto your souls. For my yoke is easy, and my burden is light.   **Matthew 11:29**

Read carefully through the next few chapters, and consume every word. This is not a sprint but a marathon. We want you to arrive at the feet of Jesus receiving His Rest. He has a yoke for you. A yoke is something that is fastened to your life that enables you to carry a load. Well, Jesus has asked you to come unto him and leave your burdens, meanwhile, he is attaching his yoke of rest to your life, and it is easy and light. This yoke speaks of an anointing of Rest which destroys every other yoke. As you take his yoke, you will become a carrier of His Rest.

And it shall come to pass in that day, that his burden shall be taken away from off thy shoulder, and his yoke from off thy neck, and the yoke shall be destroyed because of the anointing.

Isaiah 10:27

Christ's Glorious Rest will gently manifest upon and within your life as you "take his yoke", the anointing of Rest, and learn of him. By doing this you will find rest for your souls...Literal, tangible yoke destroying Rest. Chew slowly, and digest his truth.

MEDITATION

In the previous Chapters

- We have established that God created us to live in His Rest and His Order

- That Knowledge and Fear have been used by the enemy of our souls to remove that Rest, leaving humanity in a state of chaos and unrest

- That Fear is a criminal

- That Fear is unconstitutional within the Kingdom of God

- That we need to filter all incoming knowledge with the Wisdom (Word) of God, etc.

- That we have been in a war, but there is coming a shift in the momentum. You are about to enter into the REST ZONE.

The next few chapters are an invitation into an actual encounter with the Lord Jesus Christ and His Rest...
Chew Slowly...Be Patient...

REACH FOR THE ANOINTING THAT ARRESTS ALL FEAR

REST: The Root Solution

(It is essential to the manifestation of many promises, it is foundational for the release of various anointing's)

Quite often as Christians we are guilty of looking at the scriptures independent of their context, or *the conditions for which they may be fulfilled in our lives.* We often tell people what the Bible says, or what the Bible says we should be doing or not doing, experiencing or not experiencing, without ever giving them a Root Solution (a roadmap to success).

A root solution is to any common scripture, much like a root word is to any common word. For instance, the word reality is derived from the root word...real (having verifiable existence)... The word dynamic is derived from the root word Dunamis (a Greek word meaning explosive, miraculous power)...In other words, the purest form of any word is revealed by its root word...

Every word is given substance support and validity by its root. It is my firm belief that every verse of scripture is supported and validated, given power strength and ability by a root scripture. These root scriptures are the **Key** to **Unlocking** the **Secrets** to living and walking out every other scripture found in the Word of God.

Rest is a spiritually alkaline state. A state of being, where the whole man can flourish, spirit, soul and body. Rest is foundational to the Kingdom of God, and is the birthplace of peace.

Peace in its purest form is not responsive, it's creative...This is the Peace that comes from the Prince of Peace. We often relate to peace, as something we need to bring us back to soundness, back to Rest. Rest is the original state of things before the fall of man... Most of us only know peace as a response to a problem or war, as an emotion that stills our hearts, but when we speak of Rest, we are not talking about a temporary fix, we are talking about a shift in position and authority! *A n d the same day, when the even was come, he saith unto them, Let us pass over unto the other side. And when they had sent away the multitude, they took him even as he was in the ship. And there were also with him other little ships. And there arose a great storm of wind, and the waves beat into the ship, so that it was now full. And he was in the hinder part of the ship, asleep on a pillow: and they awake him, and say unto him, **Master, carest thou not that we perish?** And he arose, and rebuked the wind, and said unto the sea, Peace, be still. And the wind ceased, and there was a great calm. And he said unto them, Why are ye so fearful? how is it that ye have no faith? And they feared exceedingly, and said one to another, What manner of man is this, that even the wind and the sea obey him?*

Mark 4:35-41

CHRIST AT REST is in the ship asleep...the disciples are afraid and fearful. Out of Rest Jesus sends Peace (a Kingdom Dominion) into a storm and stills it. He is Rest, and his anointing flows in and from Rest. Out of unrest the disciples speak fear and doubt *"Master carest thou not that we perish"*. They interpreted Christ's Rest as an inappropriate response to danger, but it was that very Rest that empowered the Dominion of Peace.

This Rest/Order of the Kingdom of God is coming to the believing ones to establish the Rest of that Kingdom within. Rest brings restoration or restored order. There can be no order where there is unrest. The pre-sin order of man was Rest, and man left that position. Jesus is our Rest, and all who come to him may be restored to that position of Rest. Sabbath's, Holy Days, and Feasts of old, were all shadows and types of the true holiness, order and rest found in Jesus Christ. Holy and Righteous ordinances they are, yet only a shadow of the true!

When God Rested on the Seventh Day, this Rest was a beginning, not an ending...Rest is foundational to God's purpose for creation. We were created to live and labor, to love and worship in Rest. It wasn't until Adam sinned that he would have to work by the sweat of his brow. Ever since then, mankind has been seeking Rest.

And I said, Oh that I had wings like a dove! for then would I fly away, and be at rest.   **Psalms 55:6**

The Rest of God is more than a place or state of being, an atmosphere or a labor free zone...for us today, it is the person of Jesus Christ and his every provision, accomplishment and completed assignment on our behalf, the Lamb slain from the foundations of the world...the absolute result of God's Love.

COME UNTO ME..., AND I WILL GIVE YOU REST
MARK 11:28

God's Rest is closely related to His order. It was the slaying of a single Lamb that procured this restored order on behalf of mankind. From the foundations of the world, Jesus Christ, The Lamb of God, was provided by Love, which provided the Blood, which provided the Mercy, which provided the Grace to come and receive his Rest. It is when we are in alignment with Jesus Christ that this anointing of Rest is imparted unto us. This begins with a simple "Coming unto him"...a simple invitation to receive Christ from whom Eternal Life and the release of every Kingdom anointing flows. This Rest comes from him and out of him, not only by him. He is the unlimited source of God's true Rest. There is, though, a further application of this "coming".

As believer's and recipients of Eternal Life, I see every Kingdom attribute in its purest form when it is coming out of Rest. In other words, whether we are praying, fasting, studying, worshiping, contending in spiritual warfare, interceding, giving, loving, laughing or crying, we will always maximize our effectiveness if we are doing it from a place of Rest. Rest destroys anxiety and neutralizes fear. It frees our spiritual, emotional and physical resources to attend to the task at hand! Rest is a divine substance, given by God to His sons and daughters as a spiritual inheritance. Entering into this rest is secondary only to this rest entering into you!

I impart the Gift of faith that you may be able to receive the Rest of God at the feet of Jesus...Reaching out by faith to the person of the Lord Jesus Christ...and receiving His Anointing of Rest...He says come unto me...SIMPLE, take him literally, and tell him that you are coming, now close your eyes and exercise your faith to reach for him. This is the way to manifested rest, which neutralizes all fear. Now wait, and tell him again that you are coming for his Rest. Use your faith to reach for him, he is reaching for you. Cut off every distraction, there can be no phones, no television, no music...you are coming to Jesus, the Rest of God, the restorer of order, who destroys everything rooted in you from the tree of the knowledge of good and evil. He wants to neutralize everything that can be used to bring you unrest.

COME UNTO ME I AM REST, I AM THE ANTIDOTE FOR FEAR AND ANXIETY. WHEN YOU TOUCH ME, AND I TOUCH YOU, FEAR WILL FLEE AND CEASE

The Root Scripture for neutralizing all fear is Matt 11:28...Come unto me...

Jesus told the Rabbi's of his day that they should search the Scriptures...because they testified of Him... Whenever you find a scripture that testifies and ministers the life of Jesus Christ, you should meditate upon it until it becomes your reality. The Mystery or Root Solution to virtually every promise, in every covenant, and every epistle, is found in the Gospels in the teachings of our Lord Jesus Christ...This is why we should all spend time there before delving into the rest of the New Testament. But this cannot be a timeshare, or a hurried moment, remember, you are coming to Jesus as you search the scriptures. Everyone who found Jesus and reached out to him in faith was healed of all their diseases [diseases].

For we which have believed do enter into rest, as he said, As I have sworn in my wrath, if they shall enter into my rest: although the works were finished from the foundation of the world.

Hebrews 4:3

Jesus was the Lamb slain from the foundations of the world. He was the Lamb (in type) that Abraham found caught in the thicket, sacrificed as a substitute for Isaac. He was the Lamb (in type) that the priest's of old slaughtered for the sins of men. He is the Lamb of God who takes away the sins of the world. Believe on the Lord Jesus Christ, HIS REST IS GLORIOUS!

Unbelief affects the receiving of rest.

.... and they to whom it was first preached entered not in because of unbelief.

Hebrews 4:6

IMPARTATION: Out of the Rest of God I declare and impart to you the anointing of faith to receive the very Rest of God in the person of Jesus Christ. Receive the Rest of the Lord Jesus Christ.

HIS REST IS GLORIOUS

Testimony of my encounter with His Rest

And in that day there shall be a root of Jesse, which shall stand for an ensign of the people; to it shall the Gentiles seek: and his rest shall be glorious.   **Isaiah 11:10**

I would compare fear and anxiety this way. For me, fear is like an earthquake with sudden and grave impact, while anxiety is like the tremors and aftershocks of the earthquakes, that are less intense but can be more prolonged (a continuous state of emotional unrest)....If fear is described as a tormentor, than I would describe anxiety as an agitator.

Pressure points in life that produce anxiety are like faults that are weak points in the earth's crust. Should an earthquake hit directly on a fault, the effect would be untold. A fault is a crack in the Earth's crust along a certain geographic line.

Many of us have cracks or faults within the fragile regions of our souls. Life pain, pressure and traumas of every kind can produce these fractures, (places of weakness and vulnerability). These oppressions can be very damaging both physically and emotionally. When a person is in such a fragile state, any additional pressure can rattle them to the core. I so feel the heart of God in this moment to say to you that are hurting "My Kingdom is an Everlasting Kingdom, My Word is infallible, My Eyes are upon you,

I AM here to give you Rest"

...As that Word welled up in my spirit, I was reminded of my own initial encounter with His Rest, I will surely never forget it.

It was an early afternoon while I was rereading some of my spiritual notes on Rest. That day, I was quickened to apply what I was reading. I remember that my faith arose to a level of great expectation, and I was eager to meet the Lord. I had been in a long battle with fear, and was in the late rounds of the fight. Although I was standing my ground, I was not winning the battle. Fear had struck me blow after blow, and had begun to take its toll on my soul. I am sure that it was the Holy Spirit that directed me to read my own notes that day. While I was reading, the reality that I could touch the Lord as easily as I could turn on a light switch arrived in my spirit. So I got up, and went and laid down on my side in quietness. Shortly after this my cell phone rang, and my spirit was grieved at the interruption. Who was calling me at a time like this? Make sure that you remove all distractions when you approach the Lord to obtain His Rest.

As I laid there, I simply said "Lord, I am coming for your Rest". After waiting for two or three minutes, there were no fireworks of rest that I could recognize, but my faith was fixed on him. "Lord, I'm coming for your Rest", I repeated, and again there was nothing to speak of in terms of a change in my state of rest or peace. Now at this point, many of us would just give up, saying to ourselves "He didn't really mean that I should come unto him, and that he would literally give me rest", or "This may work for some people, but it won't work for me". Well, these statements are born from unbelief. Remember, unbelief stops us from entering into the promise of Rest. I was encouraged by my own notes, as you are being encouraged by this book, to come to Jesus for his literal Rest. Make sure to follow my example as you continue to read...

That ye be not slothful, but followers of them who through faith and patience inherit the promises.   **Hebrews 6:12**

Well, I must say that although nothing seemed to change, my faith was still at a very high level of expectation. With the support of this new found faith (which came through reading my notes, containing the Word of God), I said it again, "Lord Jesus, I am coming for your Rest". As I said this, I **reached** for him as an act of faith with my total inner being, spirit and soul in one accord. While reaching, immediately I arrived at the feet of Jesus Christ. He was not in my room, that I know of, it was as if I had been brought into the chambers of the King. All I needed to do was come. I didn't speak a word, nor do I remember him speaking. All that I can say about this encounter was that "His Rest Is Glorious"! I was infused from head to toe with a substance so wonderful, so overwhelming, so transforming, so neutralizing to everything that opposes it, that I did not want to move or leave. I actually lost consciousness of everything that I needed emotionally, I had no prayer requests. Rest had dealt with all things, and brought order where there once was chaos.

I had great peace, but it was more than peace...it was as if I was living in a garden called Eden, before the age of knowledge, naked and unashamed.

After what was probably no more than a half an hour, I remember getting up from my bed a free man. But more than free, I was filled and surrounded by the Rest of God. My perceptions of time and space were altered. My sensitivities were heightened and maximized. As I prepared to take my daily walk, everything seemed to slow down to a snail's pace. While walking, it literally seemed as if the cars were travelling at 15 miles per hour, and that time was running at half-speed. I was moving under the Dominion of Rest, and the Dominion of Fear had been broken and removed.

This encounter with the Rest of the Lord Jesus Christ transformed my life. It made quick work of Fear, more than could have been accomplished through a hundred hours of study, or a thousand declarations of faith. For this, oh Lord, I am forever grateful.

The Lord revealed many things to me in the days just after this encounter, and I would like to share them with you:

1.) *That I must continue to come unto to him to obtain and maintain this Rest (a key to remaining free)*
2.) *That this Rest is available to all who come to him in faith*
3.) *That His Rest could be imparted in a measure and would mani-*

*fest as an anointing for me, and I presume for anyone that goes
directly to the source, Jesus Christ*

4.) *That I am to always point people to him, in order to obtain
this rest for themselves, but that I could give them an initial measure as a literal "boost" for their soul*

5.) *Not to allow anyone to become dependent upon the measure
that was imparted to me, but to send them to the source, which is
he himself*

6. *Not to neglect coming for his Rest, so that I remain free from
the dominion of fear*

Precious reader, His Rest is Glorious, it is so real. You
were created to live a life infused by Rest, and in an environment
that is saturated by Rest. Go to a quiet place, tell Jesus that you
are coming for his Rest. Follow my example as a guide if you desire to...and *REACH FOR THE ANOINTING THAT ARRESTS
ALL FEAR. His Rest is Glorious* (***Khabod*: GLORY**)

ANXIETY

(The Current of Unrest)

Millions of precious people are taking anxiety medications and anti-depressants, prescribed to suppress the symptoms of this spiritual/emotional disease. And while they do provide temporary relief for some, most will have to remain on these medications for their whole lives. The cure for anxiety cannot be found in a prescription medication. The Cure for anxiety is Rest. It is the form of Rest that makes all of the difference. Jesus said *"Come unto me all ye that labor and are heavy laiden"*. The word for laiden in the original Greek text is *phortizo* **(to overload with ceremony or spiritual anxiety)**. The word for Rest in the Greek language is **anapouo which means "to refresh or take ease", to repose or to "exempt from"**.

The Cart before the Horse

You see, there may be times when anxiety has already gotten a foothold on us, and the admonition to *"Be anxious for nothing"* Phil. 4:6, becomes a picture of failure. When Stress is at an all time high, and scriptural references just can't seem to cut through the cares...The snare is set, the foot is in the trap, and anxiety has gripped the soul. This is when we return unto our first love, the one who Paul loved, the one who authored every verse of scripture,.. Oh, it is Jesus! Yes Jesus, who will patiently restore Rest to his beloved, removing the snares of anxiety. Brace by Brace, 'til we can once again, *"Be anxious for nothing"*.

So the order is this...First we come unto Jesus and receive His Rest, then, when we are refreshed, we assert the Rest anointing to pray, supplicate and give thanks unto God for His intervention in our lives. When Jesus comes, Rest comes.

And in that day there shall be a root of Jesse, which shall stand for an ensign of the people; to it shall the Gentiles seek: and **his rest shall be glorious**.   **Isaiah 11:10**

I am convinced that we have missed this treasure in our Christian experience. Most of us have not entered into Christ's abiding Rest. We've got to come unto him and learn of him if we are going to find rest for our souls.

During John's visitation to Heaven in Revelation 4:3, he saw the one who sat upon the throne, *"and He had the appearance of Jasper (Brightness) and a Sardis Stone (Fiery Red)"*. The meaning of the Word Sardis is "the escaping one", or those who "come out".

The Lord promises Rest to his beloved and "a way of escape" to the tempted. He causes us to escape the snare when we enter the Rest zone. This is wherever His presence is manifest. We should abide (wait) in His presence 'til we receive the Rest, and **continually come** to find Rest for our souls. After this experience in the presence of God, John most assuredly apprehended this Rest, and escaped every snare of anxiety surrounding his torturous imprisonment on the Isle of Patmos. Who could survive such an ordeal? Only one who was submerged in the Rest of the Lord Jesus Christ, and surrounded by His Glory!

Jesus invites us into His Rest, as a full proof way of escape from every snare and trap....

Declaration of Faith

Declare this with me NOW...I will, I have, I must, I can escape the snare of the enemy....Fear, you have no more dominion over me. The Almighty God, my Father causes me to escape without harm. I cry unto you Lord Jesus, Deeper in thee, Deeper in thee, 'till all that chides and discourages, bows it's ugly knee. Your Glory filled Rest is Preserving and Restoring me.

REST and the Sabbath Day

For if Joshua had given them rest, God would not have spoken later about another day. There remains, then, a Sabbath-rest for the people of God; for anyone who enters God's rest also rests from their works, just as God did from his. **Hebrews 4:8-10**

What is this Sabbath Rest then...is it exclusively the observance of one day of rest in seven, on the Seventh Day? The Sabbath or *Shabbat* is the Jewish day of rest and abstaining from all work. The Ten Commandments given to Israel, told them to remember the Sabbath and to keep it Holy. The Rest offered by having a Sabbath day has great benefits, but there is more to true rest than abstaining from work. A Sabbath Rest is a time (an experience) of resting from our labors...What are these labors you might ask? Well, they are certainly more than the work we do, or the occupation we may be involved in. They are more than our hobbies or personal interests, activities and commitments. In order for us to identify these labors completely, we must first define what labor is. Wikipedia defines Labor as; "physical or mental exertion, especially when difficult or exhausting". This serves as proof positive that work or labor includes not only physical exertion, but also mental and emotional exertion, both of which can be more taxing and draining on the body and the soul than manual or physical labor.

Now that we have identified labor as an inward and an

outward function, let's take a personal assessment of our work-loads.

Are you a person that consistently labors in your thoughts and or emotions? Do you ever experience seasons when a sort of "undercurrent of unrest" seems to be running steadily throughout your soul? I have endured these times in my own life, and they have affected the quality of my life-experience. I believe that I was generationally predisposed to some of this. I guess some would call this a "generational curse". Well, it sure wasn't a blessing to me throughout those years.

While I have known the Lord to be Wonderful, and a great Comforter, Healer and Deliverer, I had also seen and identi-fied this undercurrent of unrest in my life. Spiritual warfare and physical challenges were the source of most of the unrest, as well as various afflictions and darts from our adversary the devil. I have learned to remain fitted with The *Whole* Armor of God, as the nature of my ministry involved direct contact with demonic forces. Whenever I went to battle without *every* part of the Armor intact, I incurred a strike from the enemy. If I may give you a word of preservation: Sin stinks to High Heaven, and demons of affliction are drawn to its fragrance. Though God, our Father, is a merciful and forgiving God, the blindness and deception of sin gives demon spirits access to afflict, and doorways of distur-bance. Once these doors are closed, a prolonged time in the Rest of God will begin the process of renewal and recovery from every snare of the wicked. If you have been afflicted as result of open-ing a door to sin, just run back to the Lord and ask for his forgiveness. He'll be waiting with open arms!

Our Lord Jesus Christ said these words...*come unto me all ye that Labor...* **Matthew 11:28.** Jesus is our Rest from Labor!

Allow the day or days that you use as your Sabbath to be spent in communion with him. Let it be a real, intimate communion in the Rest of God, that revitalizes every aspect of your creation. God has been leading me to take Saturdays as my day to come unto Jesus for Rest. As I come unto to him, I exercise my spirit and soul to reach for him...This is preventative and restorative to my body and my mental and emotional health, as well as, a time of wonderful fellowship with my Lord. The Rest of God is the optimal environment for Healing and Miracles. Remember, His Rest is Glorious (Glory)!

MEDITATION

The Life and Times of the Prophet Elijah have much to teach us about Fear and Rest

I don't know about you, but I have gotten myself into a few bad situations because of my own poor decisions. Have you ever felt like you were suffering because of your own stupidity? Likewise, there are also times when the warfare heightens because you're doing everything right. One common concern during times of trial is the feeling that we may have failed God in some way, and have connected that failure to the trial we may be going through. Join the club, we've all been there.

As you read through the next few chapters, you will see that the Prophet Elijah was totally dependent on God for any level of success in life and ministry! Fumbles, failures, fears and foibles are all a part of the human experience, but God is faithful through it all...Read and see how God ministers His Rest to the most powerful Prophet in the Old Testament, and takes him from Trial to Triumph!

PROPHETIC DEPENDENCE

We can depend on our God

And Elijah the Tishbite, who was of the inhabitants of Gilead, said unto Ahab, As the LORD God of Israel liveth, before whom I stand, there shall not be dew nor rain these years, but according to my word. And the word of the LORD came unto him, saying, Get thee hence, and turn thee eastward, and hide thyself by the brook Cherith, that is before Jordan. And it shall be, that thou shalt drink of the brook; and I have commanded the ravens to feed thee there.   **1 Kings 17:1-4**

Elijah, here, declares to King Ahab that it will not rain these years, except it be according to *HIS* Word. This authority has clearly been given to him by God, to stop the rain, but it is God's direction, provision and providence that keep the Prophet alive during the years of this prophecy. Without this direction and providence, Elijah would have fallen victim to his own words!

This same providence is available for believer's today...Faith for this providence comes through surrender to the providential hands of Love from our Father. The truth is,....if we really knew, and could retain, the Love that our Father has for us,...we wouldn't fear anything.

Or what man is there of you, whom if his son ask bread, will he give him a stone? Or if he ask a fish, will he give him a ser-

pent? If ye then, being evil, know how to give good gifts unto your children, how much more shall your Father which is in heaven give good things to them that ask him? **Matthew 7:9-11**

One simple, yet profound truth we need to always remember is that God gives good gifts to His Children. It is when we are in the hard places of life, that this truth is hardest to believe. One way to be reminded of God's goodness towards you is to journal your victories; those overcoming testimonies never fail to encourage the soul. I personally keep a record of virtually every word, song, vision, visitation, dream, prophecy, confirmation, miracle, healing and intervention I have received from the Lord...These, for me, spell out in clear language, God's providential love towards me. They represent His personal touch in my life.

Believe in God's goodness, and bring God into remembrance of His Word. Be proactive and declare His protection, deliverance, healing, dedication, provision, intervention, and responsive Love towards you. Be intimate with Him, draw near, press into His Love, and surpass all knowledge based fear. He will meet you in the press, He will carry you to safety.

Our God never changes, He is as sufficient to us today,

as He was to the Prophet Elijah. Trust in Him,

cry out to Him. He has a special interest in your life.

You can depend on Him, *REACH*

ELIJAH

1 Kings 18

Prophetic Assignments

And it came to pass after many days, that the word of the LORD came to Elijah in the third year, saying, Go, shew thyself unto Ahab; and I will send rain upon the earth. And Elijah went to shew himself unto Ahab. And there was a sore famine in Samaria. And Ahab called Obadiah, which was the governor of his house. (Now Obadiah feared the LORD greatly: For it was so, when Jezebel cut off the prophets of the LORD, that Obadiah took an hundred prophets, and hid them by fifty in a cave, and fed them with bread and water.)

This Jezebel, the wife of Ahab (to whom Elijah was sent), was enabled and controlled by a ruling spirit of terror which struck fear in the hearts of, and disabled the power of many of the Prophets of the Lord in that day. A bewildered group of anointed vessels, once confident and assured as instruments of the one true God, had to be hidden away for fear of losing their lives at the hands of the woman Jezebel. Where was their God in all of this? How could the spiritual climate take such a turn for the worse? God had not left them; they were simply encountering something beyond their frame of reference in the realm of Spiritual Warfare.

When a person is battling the Spirit of Fear, they are encountering high level spiritual warfare. Fear is a merciless Spirit of Captivity that can be fed and fueled by introducing old and new evidence to the (5) five senses. Our five senses were undoubtedly the second mechanism for awareness and relationship before sin entered into the world. Our uninterrupted connection to God was our first source of awareness, evidence and security in the earth. Thus, we were protected from fear, because God was so near. His Glory surrounded us and became the covering for our nakedness. His Love communicated to us, Spirit to spirit, heart to heart, mind to mind, all we needed to know at any given time.

It is quite evident in both the Old and New Testaments that there are times of sovereign intervention and rescue, but many of the battles fought on the prophetic front lines have to be contended for through the use of every available spiritual weapon and resource. In this case, a wave of terroristic oppression overwhelmed the prophetic community and brought great distress to the Kingdom of God. Prophetic and Kingdom confrontations are abounding in this day also. Evil has "stepped it up a notch", and status quo Christianity will not protect the ill equipped. The Church has everything it needs to overcome evil in our day, but has in a very real way...lost its will to fight, and abandoned the pursuit of "Revelation for the Present Day". It is my sincere hope that this book will provide this "Present Day Revelation". One Word of Prophetic Revelation can turn the tide on satanic intimidation and Jezebel spirits of fear and torment. Remember that you are not alone, if God sent you, He'll back you up!

PROPHETIC CONFRONTATION

Resist the Resistance

And it came to pass, when Ahab saw Elijah, that Ahab said unto him, Art thou he that troubleth Israel?   **1Kings 18:17**

Here we see that the nation of Israel is in division again in the ranks of its leadership. The King is calling the prophet a trouble maker, which usually means that the prophet is speaking against the ungodly actions of the King. Both Prophet and Priest were called to uphold the spiritual standards of the nation, and all good Kings complied. But Ahab was a wicked King.

And he answered, I have not troubled Israel; but thou, and thy father's house, in that ye have forsaken the commandments of the LORD, and thou hast followed Baalim. **God has sent His prophet to confront the wicked King Ahab** *Now therefore send, and gather to me all Israel unto mount Carmel, and the prophets of Baal four hundred and fifty, and the prophets of the groves four hundred, which eat at Jezebel's table. So Ahab sent unto all the children of Israel, and gathered the prophets together unto mount Carmel.. And Elijah came unto all the people, and said, How long halt ye between two opinions? if the LORD be God, follow him: but if Baal, then follow him. And the people answered him not a word.* **1Kings 18:18-21**

Confrontation will be unavoidable in this life if we are going to stand for the Kingdom of God in these last days. Backlash, persecutions, satanic retaliation, darts, arrows, anchors, witchcraft, resentments, ridicule, and all manner of spiritual warfare is waged against those who are actively serving the Lord. As we are seated with Christ (our Rest) in heavenly places, we will wage war from that position, by the Authority of the Kingdom of God, and our Lord Jesus Christ. There is no power in heaven or in earth that can prevail against us when we are properly aligned and positioned in Rest.

The Kingdom of God is synonymous with Rest. In Rest, every faculty of our nature, and every resource of our being becomes available for use in real life situations. Every other anointing and gifting gets elevated and maximized in Rest, especially when we are confronted with opposition. The *Healing* anointing is benefited immensely by the manifestation of Rest, and is increased in power and potency by it. The responses of Rest are empowered by the Kingdom of God; the reactions of unrest are empowered by fear. *REACH* (for the Rest of God) before you react, and remember that you are not alone!

*And hath raised us up together, and made us **sit together** in heavenly places in Christ Jesus:*   **Ephesians 2:6**

THIS IS A PLACE OF POWER & PROTECTION
PLEASE BE SEATED

PROPHETIC DECLARATION

1Kings 18:22-29

Then said Elijah unto the people, I, even I only, remain a prophet of the LORD; but Baal's prophets are four hundred and fifty men. Let them therefore give us two bullocks; and let them choose one bullock for themselves, and cut it in pieces, and lay it on wood, and put no fire under: and I will dress the other bullock, and lay it on wood, and put no fire under: And call ye on the name of your gods, and I will call on the name of the LORD: and the God that answereth by fire, let him be God. And all the people answered and said, It is well spoken.

And Elijah said unto the prophets of Baal, Choose you one bullock for yourselves, and dress it first; for ye are many; and call on the name of your gods, but put no fire under. And they took the bullock which was given them, and they dressed it, and called on the name of Baal from morning even until noon, saying, O Baal, hear us. But there was no voice, nor any that answered. And they leaped upon the altar which was made. And it came to pass at noon, that Elijah mocked them, and said, Cry aloud: for he is a god; either he is talking, or he is pursuing, or he is in a journey, or peradventure he sleepeth, and must be awaked. And they cried aloud, and cut themselves after their manner with knives and lancets, till the blood gushed out upon them. And it came to pass, when midday was past, and they prophesied until the time of the offering of the evening sacrifice, that there was neither voice, nor any to answer, nor any that regarded.

This kind of authority is what's been missing in the end-time Church. We have traded programs and gimmicks for power and authority with God. But I do believe that there is coming a return of true Apostolic and Prophetic Power to those that have been processed unto an equivalent level of humility. A place of actual authority under Christ to cooperate with and administer the Master's end-time plans with the Voice of Elijah...John the Baptist was given that Voice of declaration to point to the Lord Jesus Christ. Chosen vessels in this day will carry this Voice of Authority, pointing the way to Jesus Christ. If you can REACH Jesus, you will never lose a battle with fear!

PRAYER: Father we ask you to give us a voice that will declare your desired message in authority and power. A Voice without Fear! A Voice declared from a position of Rest & Glory!!

PROPHETIC DEMONSTRATION

1Kings 18:30-46

And Elijah said unto all the people, Come near unto me. And all the people came near unto him. And he repaired the altar of the LORD that was broken down. And Elijah took twelve stones, according to the number of the tribes of the sons of Jacob, unto whom the word of the LORD came, saying, Israel shall be thy name: And with the stones he built an altar in the name of the LORD: and he made a trench about the altar, as great as would contain two measures of seed. And he put the wood in order, and cut the bullock in pieces, and laid him on the wood, and said, Fill four barrels with water, and pour it on the burnt sacrifice, and on the wood. And he said, Do it the second time. And they did it the second time. And he said, Do it the third time. And they did it the third time. And the water ran round about the altar; and he filled the trench also with water. And it came to pass at the time of the offering of the evening sacrifice, that Elijah the prophet came near, and said, LORD God of Abraham, Isaac, and of Israel, let it be known this day that thou art God in Israel, and that I am thy servant, and that I have done all these things at thy word.

Hear me, O LORD, hear me, that this people may know that thou art the LORD God, and that thou hast turned their heart back again. Then the fire of the LORD fell, and consumed the burnt sacrifice, and the wood, and the stones, and the dust, and licked up the water that was in the trench. And when all the people saw it, they fell on their faces: and they said, The LORD, he is the God; the LORD, he is the God. And Elijah said unto them, Take the prophets of Baal; let not one of them escape. And they took them: and Elijah brought them down to the brook Kishon, and slew them there. And Elijah said unto Ahab, Get thee up, eat and drink; for there is a sound of abundance of rain.

This demonstration of power was done for the sole purpose of magnifying the One True God, and displaying His abilities. This was not the Elijah hour; this was the Lord's time to shine! The life-style/nature of most Old Testament Prophets was an isolated one. There was very little in the way of spiritual support groups or systems for leaders, so the prophet of old had to lean very heavily upon the Lord. It is very apparent here that Elijah was sold out for God. To stand against so many false prophets at one time was an act of sheer Kingdom Courage.

After such a lengthy and furious spiritual battle as this, Elijah was surely drained and vulnerable. This should have been a time of Rest for the Prophet, but the forces of darkness rarely lie down after experiencing a defeat of this magnitude. Learning to live in the Rest of God, and making it our daily practice to come unto Jesus to receive a renewed measure, is a Kingdom Essential!

Balance and Rest are essential to remaining free from fear, especially for those who are on the spiritual front lines.

WEAKNESS and REST

Running on empty

And Ahab told Jezebel all that Elijah had done, and withal how he had slain all the prophets with the sword. Then Jezebel sent a messenger unto Elijah, saying, So let the gods do to me, and more also, if I make not thy life as the life of one of them by to morrow about this time.

And when he saw that, he arose, and **went for his life**, *and came to Beersheba, which belongeth to Judah, and left his servant there. But he himself went a day's journey into the wilderness, and came and sat down under a juniper tree: and he requested for himself that he might die; and said, It is enough; now, O LORD, take away my life; for I am not better than my fathers.*

1Kings 19:1-4

There is clearly a connection here between Rest and spiritual power. We noted that Elijah's victory over the four hundred and fifty Prophets of Baal was powerful and demonstrative. But, this kind of Spiritual battle would easily zap the strength of any earthen vessel. The threats of Jezebel, as retaliation for the death of the Prophets of Baal, came at a very inopportune time for Elijah. Jezebel threatened a weary, embattled prophet, who thought that he was the only one in Israel who had not bowed His knee to Baal. Depleted and Depressed, Elijah ran for his life.

The Words of Jezebel had much more resolve than those

of the prophets of Baal, she was the Prince over them in the material and spiritual realms. This was a threat from the heart of Satan himself, who had suffered a great defeat at the hands of this Prophet. She had risen in boldness to defend her territories, and is fearless in her resolve declaring *"So let the gods do to me, and more also, if I make not thy life as the life of one of them by to morrow about this time"* **1 Kings 19:2**

At this point Jezebel has overcome the Fear of Death and is Challenging Death itself! *"So let the gods do to me, and more also"*, says Jezebel with a fearless resolve. This is the final frontier for the end-time Church. As terrorists fearlessly flaunt their murderess practices, and the love of many waxes cold, as persecution against Christians arises around the globe, and perilous times manifest before our very eyes, many believers are retracting their confessions of faith in Christ and hiding for fear.

Men's hearts failing them for fear, and for looking after those things which are coming on the earth: for the powers of heaven shall be shaken. **Luke 21:26**

Elijah's fear was two-fold. It was a knowledge based fear (a Knowledge Trap), and it was the Fear of Death *by suffering. Both fears were based on the practices of Jezebel.* We are going to address the fear of death first, and then we will address Knowledge Traps in detail in the coming chapters.

God is faithful to bring us into His Rest, and this environment of Rest is the very environment for Healing and Angelic Encounters....

*And he looked, and, behold, there was a cake baken on the coals, and a cruse of water at his head. And he did eat and drink, and **laid him down again**. And **the angel of the LORD** came again the second time, and touched him, and said, Arise and eat; because the journey is too great for thee. And he arose, and did eat and drink, and went in the strength of that meat forty days and forty nights.* **1 Kings 19:6-8**

Thanks be to God for the ministry of angels, they are known for strengthening God's people in times of weakness

PRAYER:

Lord, we just want to pray for all of the Servants of God who are on the front lines, and for those sons and daughters who have been through the fire, the flood and the flame. May the Rest of the Lord Jesus Christ refresh you, and the angels of God come to your aid. As in the days of Elijah, so shall the Lord send angelic help to the heirs of salvation. Father, as each of your sons and daughters experiences times of occasional weakness, we ask you to strengthen them through your Rest!

Who is weak and I am not weak... **2Corinthians 11:29**

THE GOD of ELIJAH
&
THE ELIJAH of GOD
The Residue of Fear

The Prophet Elijah stood above all prophets in his day in respect to the working of miracles and the demonstration of God's power. Here we see the Prophet calling down fire from heaven again...While some prophets received abundant revelation and authored books, this prophet received power, and had books written about his exploits...

Then Moab rebelled against Israel after the death of Ahab. And Ahaziah fell down through a lattice in his upper chamber that was in Samaria, and was sick: and he sent messengers, and said unto them, Go, enquire of Baalzebub the god of Ekron whether I shall recover of this disease. But the angel of the LORD said to Elijah the Tishbite, Arise, go up to meet the messengers of the king of Samaria, and say unto them, Is it not because there is not a God in Israel, that ye go to enquire of Baalzebub the god of Ekron? Now therefore thus saith the LORD, Thou shalt not come down from that bed on which thou art gone up, but shalt surely die. And Elijah departed. And when the messengers turned back unto him, he said unto them, Why are ye now turned back? And they said unto him, There came a man up to meet us, and said unto us, Go, turn again unto the king that sent you, and say unto him, Thus saith the LORD, Is it not because there is not a God in

Israel, that thou sendest to enquire of Baalzebub the god of Ekron? therefore thou shalt not come down from that bed...

Prophets were often either loved or hated respectively, depending upon the word which they were called to deliver. The Prophetic Office undoubtedly carried with it great pressure when the prophet was unwilling to compromise the Word of the Lord. Because of this, ***God was obliged to protect His faithful prophets***, and endue them with power. After Elijah sent the word of the Lord to the king by his own messengers, the king required Elijah to come down to see him. On three occasions he sent fifty men to escort Elijah back to his court, but Elijah refused to go. And the first two times Elijah called down fire from heaven and consumed the fifty.

Behold, there came fire down from heaven, and burnt up the two captains of the former fifties with their fifties: therefore let my life now be precious in thy sight. And the angel of the LORD said unto Elijah, Go down with him: be not afraid of him. And he arose, and went down with him unto the king.

2Kings 1:14-15

This was a bold move by the prophet. It was an all or nothing move. Either God was with him or He wasn't, and obviously He was. The question is, then, was Elijah's confidence in the protection of God, or in the provision of his own (power) anointing, and there is a difference? Elijah seemed to have been given power to call down fire from heaven at will. This separates the power unto the Prophet, and does not require a relationship of trust to maintain the ability to manifest it. Though, I am sure that Elijah knew the Lord as a called Prophet would, it seems clear that the Angel was sent to give wisdom and bring light to the situation.

The angel of the Lord spoke to the Prophet about fear,...and this fear was invisible to everyone else but God. You might ask, how could someone with the power to call down fire from heaven, entertain fear? The Apostle Paul writes under the inspiration of the Holy Spirit.

But we have this treasure in earthen vessels, that the Excellency of the power may be of God, and not of us.

2 Corinthians 4:7

The Greek word for earthen here is "Ostrakinos" which means earthen ware, clay and by implication, frail. The incomparable power of God, invested in weak, frail humanity. We are all guilty of confusing this simple truth..., there is the God of Elijah, and there is the Elijah of God. The God of Elijah is Almighty; the Elijah of God is frail. The God of Elijah is Perfect; The Elijah of God is imperfect. The God of Elijah is Fearless; the Elijah of God is not fearless.

While reading of the wonderful exploits of mighty men and women of God in scripture, we tend to forget that it is the anointing and power of God doing the miracles. A note for all of

God's people…We must give as much time to "Surrender" as we do to "Splendor", and to "Intimacy" as we do to "Exploits", so that we will know in our heart of hearts that if the "Elijah of God" is in a weak place, the "God of Elijah" will arise. The angel, here, is exposing a spiritual root of fear that abode deep within the prophet's heart. Not even the mighty miracles of God could prevent this fear.

It seems obvious that Elijah was motivated by fear in destroying the "fifty's". He presumed that they had come to harm him. Self-preservation is a powerful motivator, and Elijah asserted his supernatural gifting/anointing to defend himself. Had the angel of the Lord delayed, Elijah might have called down fire on every soul, until he felt safe to come down from the mountain. One reason for this is because even though Jezebel was dead by this time, the Spirit of Jezebel was alive. Elijah's fear of Jezebel was based on the knowledge of what she had done to other prophets in her day. This fear was nothing more than a spiritual assignment against his soul. But like Adam of old, it had a great impact upon his life.

Rest and Healing are essential and necessary on an ongoing basis, not just in a reactionary way. We must take the time for ourselves to receive His Rest and recovery. The further we press into the Rest of the Lord Jesus Christ and receive His Rest, the greater its impact will be upon our lives. If given opportunity, this Rest will move into the inner regions of our souls and destroy even the very residue of Fear.

MEDITATION

In the coming Chapters we will be dealing with perhaps the
biggest Mountain of Fear yet to be conquered,
the Fear of Death,

and it's about to be removed!!!

REST: THE WEAPON OF DIVINE POSITIONING OVER FEAR

Fear can be subtle in its approach, or it can mount an all out terror campaign intent upon paralyzing vulnerable believers, and has unleashed this campaign on the Modern Day Church. Christians today will have to conquer fear, when it is encountered, in order to accomplish God's purposes in the earth for the End Times. There are four major areas of fear that have kept much of the Church in a docile, passive and defensive state in relation to the forces of darkness, and world-wide evangelism.

1. The Fear of Death
2. The Fear of Harm
3. The Fear of Disease
4. The Fear of Rejection

In this volume we will only be dealing with one of these areas of fear directly, though they are all covered somewhere in the volume of this book.

The Fear of Death (Rev 12:11)

And I heard a loud voice saying in heaven, Now is come salvation, and strength, and the kingdom of our God, and the *power of his Christ: for the accuser of our brethren is cast down, which accused them before our God day and night. And they overcame him by the blood of the Lamb, and by the word of their testimony; and they <u>loved not their lives unto the death</u>.*

Rev 12:10-11 (KJV)

The majority of the times, when we hear this scripture quoted, it is quoted without the final phrase *"and they loved not their own lives even unto death"*. This is because most of us Christians are uncomfortable with the subject of death. Or to be more specific, most of us are afraid of death itself, even though we believe in the reality of the Kingdom of Heaven, and the Resurrection of the Dead. Here, in the Western Church, we have not had to enter into this discourse about Death. We usually only deal with the subject at funerals, or when a person is deathly ill. Scarcely have we thoroughly discussed death apart from the afterlife or going to heaven. Because of this, few have had their faith exercised to oppose the Fear of Death, though they live!

I believe that there is a great mystery revealed in this passage concerning victory in spiritual warfare, which, when it is revealed to our hearts, will result in **three dimensional protection against fear.**

The last phrase in the passage quoted here in Rev 12:11 has all but become an afterthought, or point of avoidance for most Christians, but a clear prophetic message to the Church is screaming to be revealed *"and they loved not their own lives even unto death"*. This prophetic statement is a description of the end-time overcomer, and reveals the third end-time weapon given to the Saints to overcome satanic forces. This is the most powerful anti-dote for fear available to the Church, second only to The Rest of the Lord. **They loved not their own lives even unto death...**Or to put it another way, they had <u>CONQUERED THE FEAR OF DEATH.</u>

Loving not our own lives even unto death has nothing to do with dying, it is a realm of fearlessness born from the Rest of God, strengthened and weaponized by the Love of God, that sends FEAR packing!

> *... but perfect love casts out fear*   **1 John 4:8**

Self-preservation is a natural instinct, and of course in many cases God's wisdom directs this. It is not the what, but the why. Remember, victory over the fear of death has nothing to do with dying. *It is a weapon of Divine positioning in the total posture of Rest. Victory over the Fear of Death will keep us alive!* To bring it down to a very practical realm, if I saw a bunch of dogs growling and running towards me from a distance, but wasn't sure if I could make it to safety, would I make a run for it, or face them and stare them down. **Surely these dogs could smell fear, and death can too!** Adam never thought of preserving his life before he ate from the "Tree of Knowledge", he was in a total posture of Rest! Working in reverse, we will look at this third dimension of protection against fear first...and then we will take a look at the first two dimensions of protection against fear.

BREAKING FEARS DOMINION

... that through death he might destroy him that had the power of death, that is, the devil; And deliver them who through <u>fear of death</u> were all their lifetime subject to bondage.

Hebrews 2:14-15

Notice that this verse is stated in the past tense *"that had the power of death"*...

THE POWER OF DEATH... resounded in the imagination of the enemy. After the conquest of Adam and Eve, he undoubtedly held his hand high dangling and jostling the keys of death in front of the fallen angels. His greatest accomplishment to date...Death... Shortly thereafter THIS was prophesied by God right there in the Garden...

"And I will put enmity between you and the woman, and between your seed and her seed (singular); it shall bruise your head, and you shall bruise his heel."   **Genesis 3:15**

This prophecy was fulfilled when our Lord Jesus Christ, born of a woman, conquered and destroyed the devil and took back the keys of death and hell!

I am he that liveth, and was dead; and, behold, I am alive for evermore, Amen; and have the keys of hell and of death.

Revelation 1:18

Death's Power (a product of sin, a condition of separation from God, and a spiritual and physical consequence) is dependent on fear. Without fear Death has no power! Lord deliver us from the fear of Death, we have much to gain when you complete this work in us!

- The freedom to have a fearless existence
- Unabandoned boldness with power
- Greater intimacy with God
- Insight and fearless hope for eternity

When thou liest down, thou shalt not be afraid: yea, thou shalt lie down, and thy sleep shall be sweet. Be not afraid of sudden fear, neither of the desolation of the wicked, when it cometh. For the Lord shall be thy confidence, and shall keep thy foot from being taken.   **Proverbs 3:24-26**

Be not afraid of sudden fear? How could that be at all possible without the Dominion of Rest abiding within and upon our lives? God most assuredly makes these promises and gives these commandments in light of His own power over fear, and assigns this power to His people! "Lord Jesus, we are coming for your Rest"! Yes, His Rest is full of Power and Glory, just one encounter breaks fears dominion!

...God hath not given us the spirit of fear; but of power, and of love, and of a sound mind...   **2Timothy 1:6-9**

2 MORE DIMENSIONS of PROTECTION

Revelation 12:11
#1 THE BLOOD

After dealing with overcoming the fear of death, now we will deal with the first two weapons of protection against fear found in Revelation 12:11. The Blood of the Lamb & The Word of our Testimony. Many spiritual warfare volumes have been written about the Power of the Blood of Jesus Christ, because of this, I will not exhaust the subject.

The Blood of the Lamb for **Righteousness:** Right standing with God Producing (Redemption, Justification, Christ's Intercession and Advocacy)

The One who redeemed us has Justified us by "the Blood of His Cross". This legal action will stand up in the Courts of Heaven against any accusation during our trials. It is evidence of our right to pardon and protection (insuring the availability of every covenant promise). Because of this Legal Justification, He (Jesus) ever lives to make intercession [NOW] (to pray for and stand up for) our position of pardon and protection before the Father. He is our Advocate (Lawyer, the one who pleads our case, and opposes our enemies before God), the one who endorses us and preserves us through his intercession! Now that alone is an amazing Truth, but let's look a little further!

Protection: The Blood of Jesus Christ, the True Passover Lamb, gives specific power over the Angel of Death.

*"And the blood shall be to you for a token upon the houses where ye are: and when I see the blood, I will **pass over** you, and **the plague** shall not be upon you to destroy you, when I smite the land of Egypt. "*   **Exodus 12:13**

As the judgments of God were being released, He provided protection for His covenant people, when He saw the Blood! Rev 12:11 clearly reveals a continuing purpose for the Blood (of the perfect Lamb of God). Yes it justifies, yes it sanctifies, yes it cleanses...but in spiritual warfare it protects from Death and Plagues also! I believe cancer is a modern day plague. It has affected the lives of millions of people, and has become perhaps the most feared diagnosis in the healthcare arena.

The Children of Israel were instructed to place the blood upon the doorposts and side posts of their houses, visibly to distinguish them in the midst of the plague. We should have a visible faith concerning the Blood of Jesus, one that is active and fervent in displaying our confidence in its power to protect us. Yes, the Blood of Jesus Christ can protect us from modern day plagues. It is a powerful agent of Righteousness, which is a Kingdom Dominion, and in the Kingdom of God, sickness is unconstitutional!

Pray this with me: Father, Thy Kingdom come, thy will be done, on earth, in me, as it is in Heaven! I thank you for the Power of the Blood of Jesus Christ to protect me, cleanse me and preserve me. Yes, Heavenly Father, I acknowledge the Power of the Blood! I ask you to apply this to my life retroactively as only you can do. (For protection against pre-existing conditions) Yours is the Kingdom and the Power and the Glory, in Jesus name, amen.

Power: (The Spirit, The water, and The blood which agree on earth) [these each poured out of our Lord Jesus Christ while he was here in the earth and they witness that He is King of Kings and Lord of Lords]

*I saw heaven standing open and there before me was a white horse, whose rider is called Faithful and True. With justice he judges and wages war. His eyes are like blazing fire, and on his head are many crowns. He has a name written on him that no one knows but he himself. And he was clothed with a vesture dipped in blood: and his name is called **The Word of God.***

Revelation 19:11-13

He is dressed in a robe dipped in blood, and his name is the Word of God. This Robe is dipped in Blood, the Word for dipped in the Greek is *Bapto*, the root word for Baptism. It literally means to cover wholly with a fluid. This Blood has new purpose beyond redemption, and life protection, in Heaven the Blood is an agent of WAR! There is Power in the Blood!

#2 THE WORD

The Word of their testimony (to speak in agreement and in alignment with the Kingdom of God, as one who can only be tried by his own government...an ambassador). To declare the Revealed Truth, Mystery Truth, Kingdom Truth from God's Word, Voice, Visions, Encounters, Dreams, Visitations, Revelations and Experiences! This Word is not that which was brought forth from the Tree of Knowledge, but that which was brought forth from the Tree of Life...I declare over my life virtually every day that I am covered in a Vesture Dipped in Blood! This Word I received from the Lord Jesus Christ in the midst of an intense battle with FEAR.

*for he hath said, I will never leave thee, nor forsake thee. So that **we may boldly say**, The Lord is my helper, and I will not fear what man shall do unto me.*   **Hebrews 13:5-6**

Fear not; I am the first and the last:, and was dead; and, behold, I am alive for evermore, Amen; and have the keys of hell and of death   **Revelation 1:17-18**

HIS WORD IS TRUE AND CAN BE TRUSTED

WHAT is a
KNOWLEDGE TRAP?

A "Knowledge Trap" is a place of captivity to fear (a Stronghold in the mind), which was established through a particular set of learned facts, studied concepts or accepted beliefs, that are contrary to the Word of God. See if you can visualize this picture in your mind. The Human soul (Mind , Will, Intellect and Emotions) being boxed in on (4) four sides by a particular set of learned facts, studied concepts or accepted beliefs, that offer absolutely no hope for your present condition. The Soul is frantically trying to find a way out, some strand of hope for tomorrow, but the knowledge trap is secured, and the result is despair.

As a young man in my later teens, like most young men, I'd had a few experimental sexual encounters. One such encounter was with a girl who was considered easy. I was not a Christian at that point.

A few days after my scandalous experience, I ran into another friend that told me some disturbing news… He said that he had gotten a venereal disease from this same girl, some time before, and that I should get checked out. This "knowledge" became a weapon of torture in my life. I can remember feeling stupid, embarrassed, scared and trapped. How could I get checked and not be seen at the clinic? What if I had it? What's going on in my body? I was a bundle of nerves, my mind wandered towards the worst case scenarios, and the worst possible outcomes. I had no Rest at all.

After about 3 weeks of torture, I finally skipped school and set out for the clinic, looking over my shoulder with every stride. Once tested, I endured the waiting period for the results, and was delighted to hear that I didn't have a venereal disease. What a relief after such turmoil and grief, I was finally able to step out of the Knowledge Trap.

The Devil has set quite a few of these "Knowledge Traps" for me over the more recent years in my Christian life. These traps can be quite formidable if you are given to knowledge and carnal reasoning as evidence for concluding what the truth is. When I use the term "Knowledge", I am referring to limited knowledge (including the knowledge of man, carnal knowledge, theories of men, or that which emanated from the "Tree of the Knowledge of good and evil"). I am not referring to the Knowledge of the "All Knowing", "Omniscient" God., which is dressed in Wisdom, draped in Understanding, and Filtered by Love.

The Bible teaches us that we know in part.

For we know in part, and we prophesy in part.

1 Corinthians 13:9

And that there are things we do not know.

The secret things belong unto God.   **Deuteronomy 29:29**

And that God reveals unknown things!

> *But as it is written, Eye hath not seen, nor ear heard, nei-*
> *ther have entered into the heart of man, the things which God*
> *hath prepared for them that love him.* <u>*But God hath revealed*</u>
> <u>*them unto us by his Spirit:...*</u>　　　　　　**1 Corinthians 2:9-10**

While knowledge and science have provided many imme-diate benefits to mankind, the wisdom of, and or full ramification of mans inventions are often not revealed for many years into the future. It is yet to be seen, in many cases, whether the benefits out way the consequences. One such example is the advent of the mammogram, which as an agent of early prevention has provided a great vehicle for life extension to women. But most recently, multiple studies have concluded that mammograms actually cause breast cancer because of the excessive exposure to radiation used to perform the test.

Now listen, if you've had mammograms and are reading this... don't give place to a "Knowledge Trap" based on what I just wrote about recent studies! It can happen that easily! These studies, which I found out about on a popular website, may repre-sent a sincere desire to protect women, but have not factored in God's protection.

Pray this prayer with me... Father, I thank you that you have ret-roactively protected me from every harmful effect of mammo-grams and harmful radiation in Jesus name.

And these signs shall follow them that believe; In my name shall they cast out devils; they shall speak with new tongues; They shall take up serpents; **_and if they drink any deadly thing, it shall not hurt them;_** *they shall lay hands on the sick, and they shall recover.*   **Mark 16:17-18**

God's Word, here, and in many other places, declares protection from hurt. Specifically, here, this word "drink", refers to things taken into the system by mouth, skin or any bodily opening. Believe it or not, it is said that many of us drink nearly as much water through our skin when we take showers, as we do orally; and that we receive much of our supply of vitamin D through our exposure to the sun. Our skin just drinks it right in! God's word is explicit...If we drink any deadly thing, it shall not hurt us. Now, does this mean that we should throw caution to the wind, and expose ourselves to harmful things willingly, God forbid! Even exposure to the sun is reported to be harmful in excess. What are we to do then? Conflicting reports arise on almost a daily basis. We are to seek God's wisdom in everything, even when there is prevailing wisdom in place. Remember, we are not alone, he sent us the Holy Spirit to lead us and guide us into all truth. And his Word has the power to heal, cure and reverse any human condition! In every life situation, God's Wisdom prevails.

If any of you lack wisdom, let him ask of God, that giveth to all men liberally, and upbraideth not; _and it shall be given him_.
                        James 1:5

Man has been graced to make great strides through increased knowledge, because there is "good" in the tree, but this knowledge is microscopic in comparison to God's, and as stated before, without wisdom, knowledge really doesn't work. Many things that man should have "gone back to the drawing board on", we're approved, prescribed and practiced without wisdom. And, many things that should have been approved, we're withheld because they either were not profitable financially, or could not be regulated or controlled.

Today, the vast majority of the "helping systems" of the earth, whether they be Governmental, Environmental, Healthcare or otherwise, DO NOT SEEK OR ACKNOWLEDGE GOD IN THEIR DECISION MAKING PROCESSES. It is only because of God's great grace and mercy that things are not even worse on this planet, and in this country. We need God, we need to hear God, we need a touch from God, we need the presence of God, we need the Spirit of God, we need the KNOWLEDGE of GOD!

*Grace and peace be multiplied unto you through the **knowledge of God**, and of Jesus our Lord, According as his divine power hath given unto us **all things that pertain unto life and godliness, through the knowledge of him** that hath called us to glory and virtue:*   **2 Peter 1:2-3**

Grace, peace and all things pertaining to life and godliness are available to us through the knowledge of God. What does this mean, THROUGH THE KNOWLEDGE OF GOD? It means that our Lord Jesus Christ gives Kingdom access (to Kingdom Solutions) along with Eternal Life, to all who believe. It must be stated though, that, accessibility is not all that is needed to obtain its benefits. We must seek His face, and lay hold of His truth! If you are reading this book you are being enriched by Kingdom truth.

But seek ye first the kingdom of God, and his righteousness; and all these things shall be added unto you.

Matthew 6:33

Our Lord Jesus paid a heavy price so that we would not be ashamed, confounded or discombobulated (confused or bewildered). He doesn't want us groping in the darkness, without knowledge, miffed by our circumstances, overwhelmed by the enemy, crushed by present conditions. He knows what it's like to deal with oppression, he has experienced everything you are going through. He has come to end our romance with the tree of knowledge, and show us the Kingdom!

I gave my back to the smiters, and my cheeks to them that plucked off the hair: I hid not my face from shame and spitting. For the Lord GOD will help me; therefore shall I not be confounded: ... ***Who is among you that feareth the LORD, that obeyeth the voice of his servant, that walketh in darkness, and hath no light? let him trust in the name of the LORD, and stay***

upon his God.   **Isaiah 50:6-10**

When Jesus came to the earth, one of his offices was that of "Raboni" or Teacher. Even the wisest of men were astonished at his doctrine, his love, his power etc... Jesus has made more disciples than any other person in human history. Even the "winds and the sea obey him", even "the demons are subject unto his name", "how knoweth this man letters, having never studied"...You can't get this at Harvard or Yale! Jesus is the Word of God made Flesh, sent into the entire world, to be the Light of the World! The Light of Truth!

So shall he sprinkle many nations; **_the kings shall shut their mouths at him:_** *for that which had not been told them* _shall they see;_ *and* _that which they had not heard shall they consider._

Isaiah 52:15

We should be thankful for many of the good doctors and well meaning scientists (especially those that are believers) who have helped so many. And, for those "positive" advances of modern medicine, that have been graced by God to help the masses. But, we should beware of the academic romancing of knowledge; this has proven itself to be a very limiting place, a trap for the human soul. And when the human soul is trapped, "FEAR", the predator, is always lurking nearby. Fear capitalizes on "Knowledge Traps" by attempting to make man's word, equal to or greater than "God's Word" within the human heart and soul.

...yea, let God be true, but every man a liar   **Romans 3:4**

Even in his youth, Jesus discerned what he was hearing, and the Doctor's were amazed at him!

(At age 12)

And it came to pass, that after three days they found him in the temple, **_sitting in the midst of the doctors_***, both hearing them, and* _asking them questions._ *And* **_all that heard him were astonished at his understanding and answers_***.*

Luke 2:46-47

Jesus sat with, heard, asked questions, received understanding from God, and answered the doctors. This seems like a good pattern to follow concerning any path of knowledge you are considering, whether it be medical, social, political, marital, vocational, educational, financial or otherwise. Whenever possible, we should wait for understanding and answers from God before coming to any conclusions.

...Christ; In whom are hid all the treasures of wisdom and knowledge.   **Colossians 2:2-3**

The very mysteries of the Kingdom are waiting to answer every unanswered life riddle. We will have to spend more time with the Lord in these days, because the days are evil. We need to maintain an intimate relationship with the Lord, so that we can hear the wisdom and knowledge that is in him. We need an ear to hear what the Spirit is saying to the Churches. One Word from God can change the course of your life, your health, your future.

Jesus wants us to utilize the resources that he has given us access to.

Because it is given unto you to know the mysteries of the kingdom of heaven, ...   **Matthew 13:11**

Jesus was sent to open our eyes!

I the LORD have called thee in righteousness, and will hold thine hand, and will keep thee, and give thee for a covenant of the people, for a light of the Gentiles; To open the blind eyes, to bring out the prisoners from the prison, and them that sit in darkness out of the prison house.   **Isaiah 42:6-7**

Our Lord Jesus has come to free us from every "KNOWLEDGE TRAP" and the limitations of men! Do not allow yourself to remain imprisoned by what man calls "possible" and or "impossible". Jesus has come to open our eyes to the Kingdom of God, and to all of its provision. He's bringing us out of every prison, even mental prisons of defeat and hopelessness. There is no such thing as hopelessness for the Child of God, but we can believe it if we want to!

Many Doctor's today are acknowledging that people of faith heal faster than other patients, though they cannot explain this phenomenon. They are also acknowledging that plants have remarkable healing properties, whereas from the beginning, God said, ...,

Behold, I have given you every herb bearing seed, which is upon the face of all the earth, and every tree, in the which is the fruit of a tree yielding seed; to you it shall be for meat.

Genesis 1:29

...”The leaf of the tree shall be for medicine”

Ezekiel 47:12

...In the midst of the street of it, and on either side of the river, was there the tree of life, which bare twelve manner of fruits, and yielded her fruit every month: and the leaves of the tree were for the healing of the nations.

Revelation 22:2

Healing Miracle Testimony

Countless undeniable healing miracles have caused many good doctors to scratch their heads and say "Do you know how sick you were, we can't believe it, we couldn't help you". This was the case with my Grandfather, who at 84 years old was given (2) two days to live (which was downgraded to just a few hours the same day) after battling lung cancer and an orange sized tumor in his left lung (that collapsed his lung). He wasted down to 96lbs on a six foot frame, and was given up to die. As a baby Christian I went to visit him in the hospital, being born again just about three months, and laid my body over him gently, supporting my weight with my own arms. While lying upon him, I blew into his mouth (3) three times (emulating the Prophet Elijah's prayer over a child in 1 Kings chapter 17) and prayed ... "Father God, please heal my Grandfather, that they might know that the word of the Lord in my mouth is truth, in Jesus name". My prayer was adopted from this passage of scripture:

And the woman said to Elijah, Now by this I know that thou art a man of God, and that the word of the LORD in thy mouth is truth. **1 Kings 17:24**

This kind of action was completely "Out of the Box" for many of my relatives that referred to me as fanatical, and insisted that he wouldn't be healed...boldly stating in my grandfather's presence..."He's not going to be healed, he's going to die". They were stuck in the "Knowledge Trap"

I visited him every night for eight days very late in the evening, usually around midnight, so that I could pray without interruption. During this time I clearly heard the Lord speak these words "minister healing to him", and somehow I knew in my spirit that it would be like an intravenous medicine to him. I would just hold his hand and softly release healing prayers into his being, night after night...(8) Eight days later my grandfather got out of the bed and walked to the bathroom, though he fell on the way.

I knew God had healed him because he couldn't even shake my hand, much less walk. Over the next four days his improvement was astounding. He started sitting on the side of the bed with his legs crossed, and was as hungry as an ox. One day I came in and he was eating a full meal, chicken, collards, corn bread and more, which was prepared for him by a loved one. The doctor's, amazed by his improvement, released him from the hospital, and sent him to a convalescent home to die.

The convalescent home kicked him out after only two weeks saying "this man is not sick enough to be here"! When he arrived home, it was literally a "Lazarus" situation, nobody knew what to do. He was as one who was raised from the dead. He had gained weight, and even began to go out on the weekends with friends to play cards (against our better judgment). My uncle, his youngest son, suggested that he be re-examined by doctors because of his remarkable turnaround. Cancel the funeral, here comes the testimony! Upon re-examination, both Hartford Hospital, and Uconn Health Center confirmed that my grandfather was cancer free. The orange sized tumor in his left lung had not shrunk, it completely disappeared. The power of prayer in Jesus name triumphed again!

As Christians we are not to believe every spirit! We are not to believe every report! We are not to believe every wind of Doctrine. We are not to believe every Newscast! We are not to believe every Human Study, Trial or Experiment! We are not to believe every theory of man! We are not to believe everything in the text books, or the medical journals, or the newspapers. Much of this has proceeded directly from the "Tree of the Knowledge of good and evil", and as we discussed earlier, it has great power to produce fear and reduce faith. We are called to believe the Word of God! To Study at Jesus' feet, and allow the Holy Spirit to lead us and guide us into all truth. We need Kingdom Access, more than internet access! If we would spend as much time in the Word of God, as we do sitting before the words of men, we would be fearless vessels, full of fire and wisdom beholding the Kingdom of God on a daily basis!

Fear came out of the "Tree of the Knowledge of Good and Evil" and fastened itself to mans soul, his psyche. Fear, as a response or an emotion, is both inherited from Adam's original sin, and acquired through knowledge. Adam's world view was full of Faith Hope and Love before he ate from the wrong tree. Just one encounter with forbidden knowledge, changed his whole world. Be careful what you hear and what you see, the enemy of our souls, not only capitalizes on existing "Knowledge Traps", he is always trying to set new ones. If some thing, fact, data, info, word, sound byte, memory, testimony, tale, talk, trend or taunt comes into your soul that attempts to establish fear...smash it with the Word of God, and refuse to be trapped!

What you know, will either fasten itself to the fear in you, or fuel and feed the faith in you. Yes you definitely have faith! *God hath dealt to every man the measure of faith.* **Romans 12:3**

It is very important that we maintain a delicate balance in the area of man's knowledge, much of which proceeded from the

"Tree of the Knowledge of good and evil" and not from the "Tree of Life". All knowledge makes us subject to something. We see this truth spelled out in scripture.

...for by the law is the knowledge of sin. **Romans 3:30b**

When God gave the Law to Moses for the people of Israel, they immediately became subject to and accountable for keeping it. It clearly distinguished every act of disobedience to it, as sin. The Law was good and holy in and of itself, but it brought God's people under a holy scrutiny, while allowing for the priesthood to minister sacrifices resulting in temporary acts of mercy and forgiveness. The point here is that all knowledge has consequence.

Much of the knowledge that mankind is peddling as truth today is dangerously toxic to the human spirit, and in many ways directly contradicts the Word of God. It is born from a forbidden tree, and taught by the Father of Lies. If we feed on the wisdom of men, it will become a tree of knowledge within us, producing fear at every turn. The enemy of our souls thrives on carnal knowledge; it gives him a base from which to produce unbelief and doubt concerning the scriptures. While men have been graced to know in part, God is all knowing and all powerful. Without his knowledge and wisdom....failure is a sure thing, and fear will reign because of hopelessness!

We have all fallen into the knowledge trap at times, whether it came to believing the forecasted weather report, or putting all of our money into a failing commodity on the stock market, or supporting the wrong candidate, or thinking that the flu shot would actually prevent the flu, instead of creating flu like symptoms! Knowledge on virtually every subject is flooding the earth, and though some is beneficial to mankind, the vast majority of this random knowledge has one objective...FEAR!

Sex sells a bunch, and there are many things that appeal to the human condition that move people towards the point of consumption;...But fear is the greatest sales strategy on earth...Everyone from the Mechanic to the Insurance Agent uses carnal knowledge and fear to seal the deal, hey, even some Preachers resort to fear tactics to promote obedience within their respective congregations (though it is important to have a healthy fear of the Lord, the fear of man is discouraged).

Some Doctors sell diseases by fear...Have you ever heard this one..."If you don't take such and such medication, you could have a heart attack, etc.". Though, the statement may be factual, the selling point is fear. We are consuming it everywhere we go; oddly enough, many heart medications increase the risk of heart attacks, and the side effects can be more fearful than the condition itself. I am not suggesting that we ignore the advice of Doctors, only that we reject the motivation of fear. By doing this, we can remain in hope and faith for God's intervention! We, as Christians, are to be led by the Holy Spirit concerning which advice to accept, and what advice to reject. When one person is leading, the other must be following. We should always filter the wisdom of men, with the Wisdom of God.

We have all been the disciples of carnal knowledge, and subconsciously we may be relying more upon this knowledge base for the choices that we make in life, than on The Word of God. For instance, one Saturday afternoon, I banged the side of my head on the edge of my car door after picking something up off of the ground. This accident produced many painful headaches, all over my head, for over a month (though it actually jarred my memory, so that I forgot about the event that was causing my headaches). Not knowing, or remembering, where these headaches had suddenly come from, was a great source of anxiety and fear for me during those times. Each day though, I treated myself in hopes that the headaches, ear ringing and other symptoms would cease.

While complaining about my headaches to my wife, one afternoon, after consistently praying for and laying hands on myself for healing, my wife spoke these profound words to me...."Drink some water"!... I tell you, I thought to myself, "she has got to be kidding"!... "Drink some water"? "You don't get it"! "Is that all you can come up with"?... I mean, for me, it was just too simple, after all, I had prayed (which normally works wonders), taken herbs, and sought the Lord in every way I knew how. But, I did not drink water.

Eventually, after about a month and a half, I went to a doctor to have it checked out. Without health insurance (though I have a heavenly health plan), I was unable to be referred for expensive radiological tests. After a visual examination of my injury, and listening to my symptoms list, the Doctor, a very kind professional, who was a believer, diagnosed me with a mild concussion. Mind you, I had been dealing with severe headaches for over a month. Upon further examination, the Doctor discovered that my blood pressure was very elevated, and prescribed medication for it. This was surely the result of the head injury, and the stress that it was producing in my life (my blood pressure had been checked just before the injury and was almost 50 points lower). The Doctor also attributed my headaches and other symptoms to having elevated blood pressure.

Though the medication helped to reduce my blood pressure almost instantly, it did not affect the headaches or other symptoms I had been having. This was curious to me, so I started doing some web searching on my own, and as I searched the web, there was a web of fear being formed within my soul. My mind contended with numerous thoughts and fears as I ingested new "knowledge".

Could it be this? Could it be that?...Thanks be to God, I was able to cast down those invading imaginations (based in fear and In carnal knowledge), but it was a real battle, because a "Knowledge Trap" had been formed. The symptoms persisted, even in the night. Booming sounds and pains in my head woke me from my sleep, and a "Knowledge Trap" would again try to invade my thought-life. These Knowledge Traps were declaring to my mind the worst scenarios possible, and to think, I had fed on this knowledge willfully. What would I do?

Shortly thereafter, one morning while walking through my kitchen, the Lord spoke this audible Word to me ..."Drink Water"!

I heard it as clearly as any Word I have ever heard! "Drink Water"... So I filled a glass with water and drank it all, repeating this four times....That was the day that my headaches and every other head related symptom left me for good! Clearly, I had missed something that was right in front of me. My wife's words rang in my mind that day over and over. I recounted the unnecessary suffering that I had endured for over a month because I had not believed His Prophets (my wife is a Prophetess and an Intercessor). My carnal mind rejected the simplicity of the Word of Prophecy to "Drink some water", and I suffered for it.

It's time to let go of carnal reasoning, fear thrives on "what if's". Chances are that in your lifetime you've heard enough to discourage you about the prospect of finishing strong and living long. Knowledge is selling diseases like Alzheimer's for the aging, Heart Disease for the obese and Cancer to just about anyone who will buy it. Sometimes, dangerous and doubtful treatments are sold for a life savings, while patients lose everything in the process. Though the presence of these diseases within society is undeniable, the presentation of these conditions by many within the medical community is based in fear. God's Word offers real hope to the hearer, and delivers real faith to the believer. The Healing Virtue of Jesus is as real today as it was 2000 years ago.

This is the day to be engrossed with the unchanging truth of the Word of God. He is a Healer, a Counselor, a Savior, a Deliverer, a Helper, a Friend, a Lifter, a Miracle Worker, a doer of impossible things, a Rewarder of the diligent seeker, a Restorer, a

Shepherd, an Advocate, an Intercessor, a Father, a Protector, a Provider, a Revealer, a Preparer, a Peace Giver, a Defender, a High Priest, a Redeemer, our Righteousness, a Forgiver ,a Satisfier, an Upholder, a Companion, All Knowing, All Powerful, Omnipresent...There is none like Him!!!

Who is a wise man and endued with knowledge among you? let him shew out of a good conversation his works with meekness of wisdom. But if ye have bitter envying and strife in your hearts, glory not, and lie not against the truth. **_This wisdom descendeth not from above, but is earthly, sensual, devilish._** *For where envying and strife is, there is confusion and every evil work.*

James 3:13-16

We have been exposed to so much in these modern times through the media, whether it be by television, internet access, movies, advertisements, billboards or radio....Each one of these mediums can be a tool of Satan to get us into a "Knowledge Trap". Consider the vast knowledge bases of the world as an open field, with hidden land mines set in place to destroy your faith. We will need to be navigated through these fields by the Holy Spirit in order to avoid the "Knowledge Trap". In a very practical way we should be praying and asking God to lead us concerning our access to each modern day medium of information/knowledge. And we must be careful not to eat of any tree that the Lord forbids.

If we are to have complete victory over fear, we will have to limit our access to "Tree of the Knowledge of Good and Evil"

It has been said that "There is nothing to fear but fear itself", this expression seems to imply that fear (The spirit/demonic agent) has no real power except the power to produce the fear emotion. In general, I agree with this, fear almost always needs a place of reference from which to work. Fear is most often a product of what we are taught, though sometimes it is acquired generationally. This is why children, who have not inherited fear as a tendency, need our protection from unknown dangers. In many cases, they just don't know enough to be fearful. Giving our children wisdom is always encouraged, but we must be careful to limit our children's access to unfiltered knowledge, as this will greatly effect their lives.

16 WAYS to DEFEAT a KNOWLEDGE TRAP

1.) Break off your romance with (carnal) knowledge. We cannot be both "intellectual" and "spiritual" at the same time...

But he that is spiritual judgeth all things, yet he himself is judged of no man. For who hath known the mind of the Lord, that he may instruct him? But we have the mind of Christ.

1 Corinthians 2:15-16

The Mind of Christ is a mind that has and is being constantly renewed by the Word of God. Fresh waters continually flow through the caverns of thought purifying and purging the mind of fear, worry and an evil conscience. This is the mind of one (Jesus) who understood His equality with (God), but was made in the likeness of (men) [there is no measure for the distance between the two].

Christ is Wisdom personified. One who "told us things" and "showed us things" that man has never heard or seen. To be a spiritual man or woman is to ultimately side with God's Word and God's wisdom at every turn in life. It is to lean on Christ (the Anointed one), and as Christian's we have the same anointing of the Holy Spirit (though in a smaller measure) to glean truth and light from. This Light of Truth supersedes, and has the ability to counteract and contradict the very laws of nature, the very dictates of logic, and the very best conclusions drawn from the very best efforts of men.

2.) Consider God and His Word to be the foremost Authority on every subject.

Which things also we speak, not in the words which man's wisdom teacheth, but which the Holy Ghost teacheth; comparing spiritual things with spiritual.   **1 Corinthians 2:13**

While we would be wise to consider the Doctors (authorities of the sciences), as Jesus did at 12 years of age, we must allow the Holy Spirit to give us His Wisdom. It could be said that we have not really heard any conclusive thing, until we have heard from God. He knows and see's the future, and has unlimited resources to effect a desired result. His thoughts are higher than ours! Never fall into a knowledge trap. God's truth sets us free!

3.) Reject the lie, that your circumstances are proof that God has rejected you.

I will never leave thee, nor forsake thee.   **Hebrews 13:5**

God is a devoted Father to His children. If you have accepted Jesus Christ as your Savior and Lord, then you belong to

God, you are His child. King David said, *I have been young, and now am old; yet have I not seen the righteous forsaken, nor his seed begging bread.* **Psalms 37:25**...Throughout his whole life David could testify to this one truth! God never forsakes His children. The devil on the other hand, is a liar, and will stop at nothing to try to stuff this lie down your throat. Don't swallow the Lie. No matter what you've done, if you've gone to the Father, and asked for His Forgiveness, Grace and Mercy with a sincere heart, expect to see the Hand of God rescue you! Shout Amen!

4.) Remember and remind yourself, how much God Loves you.

There is no fear in love; but perfect love casteth out fear: because fear hath torment. **1 John 4:18**

Because God's love for us is perfect, it will always bring us an answer that breaks the "Torment Trap".

Then said Jesus to those Jews which believed on him, If ye continue in my word, then are ye my disciples indeed; And ye shall know the truth, and the truth shall make you free. **John 8:31-32**

When we have been spiritually and emotionally wounded by fear, we need the promises of God, given from the Heart of a Loving Father, to strengthen us, His children, in the battle. His

Word is a Love Letter to the Church. It is a Love Letter to you. In John 9:11 Jesus told a blind man to wash in the Pool of Siloam, after anointing his eyes with clay, and he received his sight. This was a detailed instruction "go and wash in the Pool of Siloam". We can all wash in the waters of God's Word. It is a pool for us to recover our sight, our vision and strength. It has a provision or promise for every life situation. Every one! Every One! Every One! Yours! Look into the Father's Love Letter, it is signed with the Blood of the Lamb, and Sealed by the precious Holy Spirit!

5.) Get Prayer for Deliverance from Evil

Finally, brethren, pray for us, that the word of the Lord may have free course, and be glorified, even as it is with you: and that we may be delivered from wicked and evil men. For not all have faith.   **2 Thessalonians 3:2**

Even the Apostle Paul knew the benefit of receiving corporate prayer from anointed and sincere brothers and sisters in the faith. He asked for prayers of deliverance from evil men. Threats of every kind, and real attempts on Paul's life were a common occurrence, but God's hand of deliverance kept extending Paul's life. Paul lived approximately 65 years, and that was considered a very long life during those days. To have lived such a long life under the constant threat of death from both Jews and Gentiles, as Paul proclaimed the Gospel of Jesus Christ, is clear evidence of God's divine hand of protection and divine supply of strength! At the end of his life, Paul was likely beheaded as a Christian Martyr, but the Lord notified him that he had finished his work, and that his time of departure was at hand. The Apostle Paul, having finished his course, crossed over into Glory, fearless, and ready to meet the Lord! Hallelujah! Undoubtedly, the prayers of the saints helped preserve this man's life and ministry!

6.) Write the Vision, Journal your Victories

And thou shalt bind them for a sign upon thine hand, and they shall be as frontlets between thine eyes. And thou shalt write them upon the posts of thy house, and on thy gates.

Deuteronomy 6:8-9

God, here, commands the Children of Israel to attach written copies of his commands to their bodies, and to the front of their houses, as a constant reminded of the covenant they shared.

The Bible itself is largely a journal of victories that God has wrought for His people over their natural and spiritual enemies. These written records, especially the record of the Exodus, and God's Deliverance of Israel from the Land of Egypt, as well as countless other victories recorded in both the Old and New Testament, serve as powerful reminders of God's intervention in the affairs of His people. I have journaled God's interventions in my life for many years, and I have found that these spiritual notes have prevented both "Torment and Knowledge Traps" from prospering against me. The written record of God's intervention increases faith, fortifies the thought-life, glorifies the Power of God and exalts God's ability over man's ability!

Jehoshaphat's Secret's ... I Chronicles 20:1-30

7.) Seek the Lord with everything you have

*It happened after this that the people of Moab with the people of Ammon, and others with them besides the Ammonites, came to battle against Jehoshaphat. Then some came and told Jehoshaphat, saying, "A great multitude is coming against you from beyond the sea, from Syria; and they are in Hazazon Tamar" (which is En Gedi). And **Jehoshaphat feared,** and set himself to seek the Lord, and proclaimed a fast throughout all Judah. So Judah gathered together to ask help from the Lord; and from all the cities of Judah they came to seek the Lord.*

It isn't "spiritually correct" today for Leaders to admit to feeling fearful. This of course does not change the reality that many of us have battled this foe at large. Even the likes of Oral Roberts, in his later years said "there have been many fearful things". This was undoubtedly because of the demonic backlash he encountered in his anointed ministry of deliverance and healing. Like Jehoshaphat, we seek the Lord and His power lifts us up to heights beyond ourselves, transforming us in the process. The more we see Jesus, the less we know fear!

8.) Declare to God and yourself His Mighty Power

Then Jehoshaphat stood in the assembly of Judah and Jerusalem, in the house of the Lord, before the new court, and said: "O Lord God of our fathers, <u>are You not God in heaven</u>, and <u>do You not rule over all the kingdoms of the nations</u>, and <u>in Your hand is there not power and might</u>, so that <u>no one is able to withstand You?</u> <u>Are You not our God</u>, <u>who drove out the inhabitants of this land before Your people Israel</u>, and <u>gave it to the descendants of Abraham Your friend forever?</u> And they dwell in it, and have built You a sanctuary in it for Your name, saying, 'If disaster comes upon us; sword, judgment, pestilence, or famine; <u>we will stand before this temple and in Your presence (for Your name is in this temple), and cry out to You in our affliction, and You will hear and save.</u>'

9.) Declare your dependency upon God, taking the weight off of yourself, casting your cares upon Him.

And now, here are the people of Ammon, Moab, and Mount Seir; whom You would not let Israel invade when they came out of the land of Egypt, but they turned from them and did not destroy them; <u>here they are, rewarding us by coming to throw us out of</u>

Your possession which You have given us to inherit. O our God, will You not judge them? For we have no power against this great multitude that is coming against us; nor do we know what to do, but our eyes are upon You."

About 7 years ago I was suffering with a stomach problem that caused me to bleed from both ends. After months of standing for healing and feeling very I'll, though I had no health insurance, I went to get checked out, and many tests later they couldn't find anything wrong with me. (Bleeding is not a normal bodily process, so I am sure that the Lord healed me in some way before I got there), but I was still experiencing the symptoms of malaise and weakness. During the time of this infirmity, I sought the Lord daily for relief and healing. As it was, our church was going on a 21 day Daniel fast. And on the 13th day of the fast, I found a little booklet written by my spiritual dad Wade Taylor called "healing and the communion".

As I read through it, I was encouraged to begin taking communion the next day. Well much to my surprise, a brother in Christ heard the Lord tell him to buy me a loaf of bakery bread, and brought it to my Job. When I opened up the bag, I saw what looked like a body, the kneaded bread looked like the abdominal area of a body having no slices and a golden crust. At that very moment, I reached into the bag and partook of the Body of Christ. After only five days of communion, I was totally healed of the infirmity which troubled me for nearly nine months. He Lord has our answers to every life-challenge.

10.) Be open to a True Prophetic Word of Direction and Instruction

*Now all Judah, with their little ones, their wives, and their children, stood before the Lord. <u>Then the Spirit of the Lord came upon Jahaziel the son of Zechariah</u>, the son of Benaiah, the son of Jeiel, the son of Mattaniah, a Levite of the sons of Asaph, in the midst of the assembly. And he said, <u>"Listen, all you of Judah and you inhabitants of Jerusalem, and you, King Jehoshaphat!</u> **Thus says the Lord to you**: <u>'Do not be afraid nor dismayed because of this great multitude, **for the battle is not yours, but God's.**'"*

The carnal mind would normally wrestle with such a statement "Do not be afraid or dismayed". It is not easy to trust God when we are facing grave danger, but our lives will surely present us with battles that are beyond our capacity to win. In this case, the Word of the Lord was "The Battle is not yours, but God's". Yes there are times when we don't even have to fight. God fights for us!

Once, while being confronted and instigated by a crowd of people that wanted to fight me because I wouldn't back down to their demands, I saw God turn the hearts of my oppressors and then imprison the main troublemaker the next day. In that battle I didn't have to lift a finger, I needed only to pray!

11.) Follow instructions received perfectly,
they will position you for Victory!

*'Tomorrow go down against them. They will surely come up by the Ascent of Ziz, and you will find them at the end of the brook before the Wilderness of Jeruel. <u>You will not need to fight in this battle.</u> **<u>Position yourselves</u>**<u>, stand still and see the salvation of the Lord, who is with you,</u> O Judah and Jerusalem!' **<u>Do not fear or be dismayed; tomorrow go out against them, for the Lord is with you.</u>"*

Follow instructions and get into position. Even though all born-again believer's have the Holy Spirit today, the New Testament Prophet, as part of the Five-Fold ministry, can be a great asset in delivering clear directives for the positioning of individuals, Churches and Ministries in the Body of Christ. The Anointed Word of a true Prophet of God, or Prophetic Instrument, will break a "Knowledge Trap" into pieces. This kind of Word is Spoken of in Hebrews 4:12 it is "Quick (alive) and Powerful".   I have been on both the giving and the receiving end of such Word's that have brought instant deliverance from fear which came by "Knowledge Traps"; perhaps because this Word also "divides asunder soul and spirit"...it separates the unstable soul, (it's thoughts, worries, fears and reasoning's) from the human spirit, so that it can attach itself to the Infallible Word of God!

Several years ago when my wife and I were trying to move into a house (renting with the option to buy), we needed to come up with a down payment of $5400.00 to move in. At that time neither of us was working, and the ministry was not paying us much at all. I had been a food vendor on the streets for years, and used it as a tool to evangelize. When a friend of mine game me a food cart for free, I couldn't pass up the opportunity, and began selling right away.

While trying to earn enough for the down payment, my wife, who was in Oregon at the time, called me and told me that the sister she was staying with, had a word for me. When the sister came to the phone she said "The Lord gave me a Word for you, put down the hot dogs and come and get some steak". Well, I'll tell you the truth, I was a little offended, doing the best I could to earn the down payment money, and to get a word like that (can you hear the pouting in my voice). I made up my mind that I wasn't going to Oregon to get some steak; I was sticking to my game plan. Well thank God for the True Prophetic Ministry!

While attending a meeting at a local church just a few days later, a visiting prophet asked me if he could give me a word. I said yes and got up for prayer...He said brother, "The Lord said that he gave you a word, and you were skeptical about it, but it was from him". Immediately in my spirit I knew what he was talking about "put down the hot dogs, yeah, yeah, yeah". I flew out to Oregon and came back with more than half the money for the down payment. God had a better plan!

12.) Worshipful Obedience & Faith Induced Praise

And Jehoshaphat bowed his head with his face to the *ground, and all Judah and the inhabitants of Jerusalem bowed be-* *fore the Lord, worshiping the Lord. Then the Levites of the children* *of the Kohathites and of the children of the Korahites stood up to* *praise the Lord God of Israel with voices loud and high...*

This was an act of surrender and submission to the Will of God, the Directives of God, the Mercies of God and the Powerful Hand of God! Praise erupted after worshipful obedience to the instruction of the Lord! Worship in the face of danger is the fruit of brokenness, dependence and reliance upon God. His eyes are moving to and fro throughout the earth seeking to show himself strong on behalf of those whose hearts are perfect towards him.

13.) Believe His Prophets, They carry His Word!

So they rose early in the morning and went out into the Wil- *derness of Tekoa; and as they went out, Jehoshaphat stood and* *said, "Hear me, O Judah and you inhabitants of Jerusalem:* ***Be-*** ***lieve in the Lord your God, and you shall be established; believe*** ***His prophets, and you shall prosper."***

God here, made direct intervention in Jehoshaphat's and

Israel's lives. Today, this direct intervention can be made through the indwelling of the Holy Spirit. Through the Holy Spirit there are 9 Supernatural Gifts and Unlimited ways in which God can use them to assist us.

During a very cloudy season in my life, when I was going through a period of sorrow, the Lord awakened me with 5 successive songs, all of which contained the word SUNSHINE. I had barely remembered hearing these songs, but all at once, one after another, the Holy Spirit brought them up in my spirit. As each one played, about 10 seconds each, I began to experience the Joy of the Lord. It was as if the Holy Spirit had manifested within me as a divine disk jockey bringing forth a glorious mix of prophetic music.

14.) The Power of Corporate Praise
Confounds the Enemy

And when he had consulted with the people, he appointed those who should sing to the Lord, and who should praise the beauty of holiness, as they went out before the army and were saying: "Praise the Lord, For His mercy endures forever." Now when they began to sing and to praise, the Lord set ambushes against the people of Ammon, Moab, and Mount Seir, who had come against Judah; and they were defeated. For the people of Ammon and Moab stood up against the inhabitants of Mount Seir to utterly kill and destroy them. And when they had made an end of the inhabi-

tants of Seir, they helped to destroy one another. So when Judah came to a place overlooking the wilderness, they looked toward the multitude; and there were their dead bodies, fallen on the earth. No one had escaped.

The anointing of praise flows effortlessly out of the anointing of Rest. As you come unto Jesus to receive his Rest, the release to praise the Lord is manifested within. This praise invites more of God's presence, angels and anointing. For where the Spirit of the Lord is there is freedom! Lord we thank you for the freedom to praise you, and the yoke destroying power of your Rest!

15.) Rejoice in the Lord for His Faithfulness

When Jehoshaphat and his people came to take away their spoil, they found among them an abundance of valuables on the dead bodies, and precious jewelry, which they stripped off for themselves, more than they could carry away; and they were three days gathering the spoil because there was so much. And on the fourth day they assembled in the Valley of Berachah, for there they blessed the Lord; therefore the name of that place was called The Valley of Berachah until this day. Then they returned, every man of Judah and Jerusalem, with Jehoshaphat in front of them, to go back to Jerusalem with joy, **_for the Lord had made them rejoice over their enemies._** *So they came to Jerusalem, with stringed instruments and harps and trumpets, to the house of the Lord.*

For every tear you've cried, for every attack you've endured, for every broken promise, abandonment and desertion, for every fear, for every symptom, for every scare tactic, for every oppression, backlash and retaliation against your life. For every slander for every mockery and ridicule, for every stripe you've received and bruise, for every injury and infirmity we command by the authority of Jesus Christ that every Enemy vacate the territories of your mind, body and soul, your substance and inheritance, your ministry and offspring, your spouse and your spiritual sons and daughters, your labors and your favors, and that the spoils be left behind to be plundered by the sons and daughters of the living God.

16.) Rest in the Lord

And the fear of God was on all the kingdoms of those countries when they heard that the Lord had fought against the enemies of Israel. **Then the realm of Jehoshaphat was quiet,** **_for his God gave him rest all around._**

Thank you Lord Jesus for surrounding us with your Glory-Rest

MEDITATION

PRAYER

In the name of the Lord Jesus Christ I command every Tormenting Spirit to release your soul from captivity to FEAR. I undo every Knowledge Trap in the Mind, and break the stronghold of every ungodly thought pattern and imagination assignment against your mind. I break the power of carnal knowledge, ever-changing facts, conclusions, reasoning's, logic, unbelief, carnal deductions, lying vanities, lying prognoses, limited wisdom, God complexes and every other micro byte of untruth or part truth inflicted upon you directly and indirectly by the influence of the Tree of Knowledge. I now release unto you the REST of the Lord Jesus Christ! Receive the REST of our Lord and Savior Jesus Christ. Repeat this with me: I receive the REST of my Lord and Savior Jesus Christ! I receive the REST of my Lord and Savior Jesus Christ. I receive the REST of my Lord and Savior Jesus Christ. Even if you have not yet accepted Jesus Christ as your Savior and Lord, he is still offering His REST to you. He is the only source for complete REST!

If you haven't already received the Rest of the Lord Jesus Christ in Glorious manifestation...It is now time to

R. E. A. C. H.

If you would like to accept the Lord Jesus Christ into your heart, just turn to page 129 of this book.

Relax Extend Access Come Heal

The Lord has invited every believer to come unto him and to receive his rest. This is more than an invitation to forgiveness, which is a part of the process, but an invitation into an actual encounter with a profound aspect of his nature, and a remarkable substance of his being...REST.

Relax; he wants you to receive this rest more than you do. The doors of love are always open, 24 hours a day you can come. There's never an inconvenient time to come, never an inconvenient hour. Rest assured, Jesus is assured Rest. Won't you come in, believe that you will receive. See yourself approaching the Lord, the details of your vision may differ from mine, he is without limitation, he is incomparable in power, transcendent and eager to meet with you...Remove every distraction, and commit to endure the process of mental and emotional distraction. The flesh is very impatient, but wait and reach. Faith and patience must partner together in this pursuit of the Lord and his Rest, so come...My son and my daughter, come,...

I call you into my Rest for the release of every burden of heart, mind and soul, Spirit to spirit I meet with you. R E A C H...Extend your heart to me, extend your faith towards me, extend your love towards me, you are approaching and entering into my Rest...Come further into my room, my bosom, my heart is oh so open to you...break the barriers of impatience, breach the barriers of intimacy and come further into my room. As you begin to receive my Rest, it will overwhelm you, endure my gift and let it consume your burdens, every fear and stress...Nothing that opposes my Kingdom can remain when you encounter my Rest, you have come into the Kingdom, you have experienced my Order and my Peace, not as the world gives, MY Peace...Overwhelmed, Overwhelmed in the presence of my Grace, Overwhelmed in the presence of your King, Overwhelmed in the presence of My Peace...

Fear, it has no power here. Fear, it has no power to afflict when you're near. So I clothe you in the presence of my Rest. So I fill you with the Glory of my Rest. You have accessed your inheritance, and every yoke of Fear is broken...

Now be purged of the residue of Fear in your members, be purged of the residue of fear in your subconscious, now be purged of the residue of fear in your dream life, thoughts and imaginations...Wash now in the presence of my Glory...I am here...surrender to my Rest, it has conquered your enemies and vanquished your fears...Come daily for more 'til all you know is Rest...As my Rest arises, do not neglect to come my child, come, and I will give you Rest...The Kingdom Dominion of Rest is fastened to your life from this very moment...It will make itself known, as it is a part of me, my abiding presence upon you manifesting in Rest...REACH, as often as you come I will meet you with a measure of my tangible Rest...COME TO THE TREE OF LIFE AND EAT of me...

A Biblical example of Reaching

And a certain woman, which had an issue of blood twelve years, And had suffered many things of many physicians, and had spent all that she had, and was nothing bettered, but rather grew worse, When she had heard of Jesus, came in the press behind, and touched his garment. For she said, If I may touch but his clothes, I shall be whole. And straightway the fountain of her blood was dried up; and she felt in her body that she was healed of that plague. **Mark 5:25-29**

The parallels are real. This is a great example for us to use for REACHING for His Rest. This woman had to press through the commotion of a frantic crowd; she had to press through the emotion of 12 years of pain; she had to press through the opinions of those who stigmatized her as unclean; she had to press through the doubt of twelve years of failure; she had to press through to revelation of the power of the priesthood; she had to press through to understanding of the gravity of the anointing flowing downward from Aaron's beard to his skirts (the Hem of his garment). Surely she understood that Jesus was greater than Aaron, his anointing unparalleled for all generations. She had to press through to healing by the power of her faith, she had to press through to her miracle, at the touch of a garment worn by a man, the Son of man, the Son of God, the Messiah, the Great Physician...

Never had there been an example of such a press, such a REACH, in scripture. She had no patterns to follow. She became the pattern, she established the precedent, that one could be healed by touching a garment...

Her press was beyond reason, beyond logic, beyond fear, beyond...and she obtained favor, and she obtained healing, and she obtained grace and mercy and comfort at the touch of a garment worn by a King. REACH and TOUCH, BELIEVE AND HOPE, RECEIVE AND HEAL...R E A C H.

CONCLUSIONS IN REST

- *REST is much more to be known than to be known about.*

- *The Anointing of REST becomes tangible as it is transferred from the anointed one to His anointed servants. They become the expression of Him, meaning the expression of the REST that He gives in Glorious Manifestation*

- *They obtain the ability to impart the REST of the Lord Jesus Christ as a type of first fruits to those that would seek the Lord for a further and deeper apprehending of it.*

- *His REST IS GLORIOUS...It manifests the Glory of God and totally disparages FEAR on every level.*

- *REST Establishes a perimeter around us within which nothing can bring unrest, and without which nothing can approach...*

- *REST Subdues and confronts fear so that we do not have to...it engages everything that opposes it.*

- *If an enemy should approach unto the REST of God, and you feel intimidated, only surrender to the REST and it will establish its own dominion over your enemies on your behalf.*

- *REST must be pursued and maintained on a daily basis to remain in full throttle. This is because it is given by measure and not without measure. We are to continually come unto the Lord Jesus Christ for the filling and the overflowing of His rest within and upon us.*

- *REACH REACH REACH for JESUS*
- *COME COME COME unto HIM*
- *RECEIVE RECEIVE RECEIVE HIS REST*

Let go of every burden and bondage to fear as the order of the Kingdom of God is manifested within and upon you. Remember Fear is judged, and is unconstitutional within the Kingdom of God. Order in the courts of your heart! You are loved; you are covered by the most powerful government in the universe, The Kingdom of God. Jesus Christ, who is our Rest, is the Prince of Peace... (The Kingdom Dominion)

For ye have not received the spirit of bondage again to fear; but ye have received the Spirit of adoption, whereby we cry, Abba, Father.   **Romans 8:15**

Acknowledgements

Special thanks to my wife Estelle, my chief intercessor, woman of faith and best friend; to my Spiritual Mentor's over the past 25 years: Wade Taylor, Jay Francis, Matthew Caruso, Herbert Rylander and other great men and women of God who played a significant role in my life; to Denise Courts, Tony Flood and Brett Tompkins for spiritual seasonings; to Basil and Roxann Robinson for Apostolic impartations; to the Master's Table family for your love and support; to Richard K. Taylor Sr., Barney Christie, Anthony Christie, and to my mother Joyce Christie-Taylor for a mother's unending love, and the gift of writing; to my children (natural and spiritual sons and daughters) and grandchildren, I release a generational blessing of spiritual life... Above all I thank my Heavenly Father for the gift of His Son Jesus Christ, my Lord and Savior, and the presence of The Holy Spirit within my life and ministry.

The Author's additional Notes on Rest

Rest is reflective of unrest. There can be unrest without war, but there cannot be war without unrest. Therefore we conclude that rest is fundamental and peace is situational. War can produce unrest, but so can disease, hunger, weather patterns, violence, financial woes etc. Peace stops wars, but they begin again and again, but when the restoration of all things is come, there will be no more war. Rest is the fruit of the Tree of Life, Peace is the fruit of the Spirit manifesting within the life of man. Peace is also a Kingdom Dominion, and is equal to Rest when harnessed by the Lord Jesus Christ; He is Ruler of both Rest and Peace.

The Bible teaches us that the *"Kingdom of God is within you (us)"* **Luke 17:21.** I believe that what Christ was teaching here was that there is a particular aspect of the Kingdom of God that manifested within every believer when we received the Holy Spirit. This can be clearly seen by this scripture: *For the kingdom of God is not meat and drink; but righteousness, and peace, and joy in the Holy Ghost* **Roman 14:7** Unlike the outward observances of the Old Testament, the Kingdom of God would now be evidenced, manifested and experienced by the indwelling of the Holy Spirit! Let's take a closer look at one of these Kingdom Dominions given to us by Jesus Christ, and discover their unlimited power to protect our lives from a fearful invasion?

*Peace I leave with you, my peace I give unto you: **not as the world giveth**, give I unto you. Let not your heart be troubled, neither let it be afraid*   **John 14:27**

Here, our Lord Jesus Christ confidently speaks of a Peace that protects the Heart from trouble and from Fear. *Peace I leave with you, MY PEACE...NOT AS THE WORLD GIVETH!* There is a magnificent mystery here that is staring us right in the face. What kind of PEACE is this that Jesus speaks of, it's the Peace that protects from trouble and Fear. Are there resources within His Eternal Kingdom that we have not fully tapped into? And, could they actually be abiding within us already? Resources like PEACE, that are "not as the world gives", or not of this world. Surely these Kingdom resources would enable us to neutralize, counter-attack and unseat the Dominion of FEAR in these last days. This PEACE that Jesus speaks of is OTHERWORLDLY-PEACE, KINGDOM-PEACE! You see, Jesus is speaking from a Kingdom perspective, not a worldly perspective.

When we think of Peace, we often think of the absence of stress, war and conflict, but our experiences with Peace have been temporary, fleeting and more illusion than reality. The Peace that Jesus speaks of is a KINGDOM DOMINION (GOD-LEVEL PEACE infused with GOD'S AUTHORITY), and Jesus Christ is the Prince over it! Dominion can be simply defined as Established Authority! This Peace has been established eternally, and is of the highest imaginable order.

I must take the time here to note one major difference between the administration of the Prophetic Office in the Old Testament versus the New Testament administration. And that is this, if the Elijah of God scenario of weakness were to occur today, there should be a Kingdom response to build up the weakened member of the Body of Christ. The Apostle, Evangelist, Pastor, Teacher or any number of Prophetic Vessels could Stand in the Gap, Stand in Agreement, Stand in Opposition, Stand in Faith, and Stand in Power against this wicked Jezebel Spirit! God had to send an Angel to refresh the Prophet, and to later visit Elijah personally. It was not until Elijah had eaten and RESTED, that he received strength for the journey. As the Body of Christ, we must learn to Stand together and pool our spiritual resources for increased power!

Just a thought for you recipients of God's Great Grace
(which came through Jesus Christ)

Peace is the atmosphere of Grace...they are often coupled within the scriptures, and Grace is the environment of Miracles....

For thus saith the Lord GOD, the Holy One of Israel; In returning and rest shall ye be saved; in quietness and in confidence shall be your strength:...   **Isaiah 30:15**

There remaineth therefore a rest to the people of God.

Hebrews 4:9

Come unto me!

UNDER THE SHADOW

Thus will I bless thee while I live: I will lift up my hands in thy name. My soul shall be satisfied as with marrow and fatness; and my mouth shall praise thee with joyful lips: When I remember thee upon my bed, and meditate on thee in the night watches. (COMING UNTO HIM FOR HIS REST) Because thou hast been my help, therefore in the shadow of thy wings will I rejoice. My soul followeth hard after thee: thy right hand upholdeth me.

PSALMS 63:4-8

Be merciful unto me, O God, be merciful unto me: for my soul trusteth in thee: yea, in the shadow of thy wings will I make my refuge, until these calamities be overpast.

PSALMS 57:1

Thy righteousness is like the great mountains; thy judgments are a great deep: O LORD, thou preservest man and beast. How excellent is thy lovingkindness, O God! therefore the children of men put their trust under the shadow of thy wings. They shall be abundantly satisfied with the fatness of thy house; and thou shalt make them drink of the river of thy pleasures. For with thee is the fountain of life: in thy light shall we see light. O continue thy loving -kindness unto them that know thee; and thy righteousness to the upright in heart. Let not the foot of pride come against me, and let not the hand of the wicked remove me. There are the workers of iniquity fallen: they are cast down, and shall not be able to rise.

PSALMS 36:6-12

We sincerely pray that His Rest is becoming your habitation

In your Rest Notes.
Write down your encounters with Christ's
Tangible Rest....it really is Glorious

I Release to you
the Rest of the Lord Jesus Christ

attend to my words; <u>*Proverbs 4:19-21*</u>*-Rest notes*

_____

_____

_____

_____

_____

_____

_____

_____

_____

_____

_____

_____

_____

_____

_____

_____

_____

_____

_____

_____

_____

_____

_____

_____

attend to my words; _Proverbs 4:19-21_-**Rest notes**

attend to my words; _Proverbs 4:19-21_-**Rest notes**

attend to my words; *Proverbs 4:19-21*-Rest notes

attend to my words; <u>Proverbs 4:19-21</u>-**Rest notes**

attend to my words; <u>Proverbs 4:19-21</u>-Rest notes

attend to my words; _Proverbs 4:19-21_**-Rest notes**

_____

_____

_____

_____

_____

_____

_____

_____

_____

_____

_____

_____

_____

_____

_____

_____

_____

_____

_____

_____

_____

_____

_____

_____

attend to my words; *Proverbs 4:19-21***–Rest Notes**

Prayer of Salvation

Lord Jesus I ask you to come into my Heart and fill my life with hope. I surrender to you Lord Jesus, and ask you to save me from my sins and fears. I believe that you died and rose again for me. I want to live for you because you died for me, thank you Lord for saving me.

Other Published Books By Richard Taylor

- ## **A Beauty Mark: The Mark of an Overcomer**

 "A Beauty Mark" is a Powerful Christian Devotional which explores and imparts the Divine perspective of beauty in weakness. As it delicately unveils our flaws (beauty marks), it asserts that God's Glory shines far brighter than does the visible flaw. It is from this perspective that the reader is encouraged to view/see ones own self and others. The Author contends that to attain perfection or flawlessness through any other means is akin to following Satan's deceptive road to independence. (History itself has taught us about the futility of mankind without God). As a reflector of God's own Light, he began to glory in his own beauty, not understanding the privilege of reflecting the beauty of God. "The Light was not his own, nor the reflection, only the privilege belonged to him". Engaging and riveting examples are taken from scripture and modern life depicting the beauty of God's embrace upon the broken and flawed. This book offers to it's readers a new pair of eyes, to embrace with God's love what was once despised. You will want to enjoy it again and again.

On Amazon.com & Barnesandnoble.com In paperback and kindle editions…

Other Published Books By Richard Taylor

- ### GALL: Overcoming the Power of Dominating Emotions

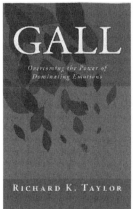 "Gall" is a victory lap for multitudes of people who are struggling with spiritual and emotional strongholds. This book exposes the spiritual root of such strongholds as Bitterness, Rejection, Shame, Self-Pity, Fear and Pride, while prescribing the appropriate antidotes. This groundbreaking revelatory masterpiece unfolds corners of untold truths for the equipping of this present generation, while presenting dynamic tools for sustained freedom from dominating emotions.

On Amazon.com & Barnesandnoble.com In paperback and kindle editions…

For
Ministry Bookings/Itinerary
Speaking Engagements/
Author Events/
Book Signings/
Call 860-206-0424
Author Website:
www.richardktaylor-author.com

Ministry Affiliation:
The Master's Table Ministries
Apostolic Leadership
Richard Taylor
(Senior Pastor/Apostolic Leader)
Estelle Taylor
(Prophetic/Pastoral)

P.O. Box 290290
Wethersfield, CT
(860) 206-0424
www.themasterslove.org

Made in the USA
Charleston, SC
16 October 2014